MISHKID
A KENYAN CHILDHOOD

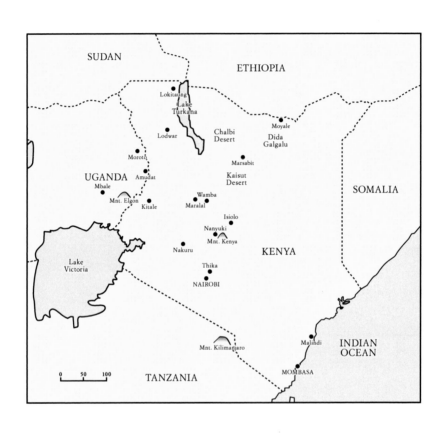

MISHKID

A Kenyan Childhood

o o o o o o o o o o o o

David Webster

Mishkid: A Kenyan Childhood
David Webster

Published by Aspect Design 2011
Malvern, Worcestershire, United Kingdom.

Designed and Printed by Aspect Design
89 Newtown Road, Malvern, Worcs. WR14 1PD
United Kingdom.
Tel: 01684 561567
E-mail: books@aspect-design.net
Website: www.aspect-design.net

ISBN 978-1-905795-88-8

To my missionary parents, Eric and Ruby,
my mishkid siblings, Dennis and Marilyn,
and my own wonderful mishkids,
Andrew, Paul, Stephen and Lynette.

CONTENTS

GLOSSARY

askari: policeman, soldier.

BCMS: Bible Churchmen's Missionary Society – an evangelical Anglican mission, now called Crosslinks.

boma: a stockade for cattle; also used of an administrative or trading centre.

chai: tea (often boiled with milk and sugar, and sprinkled with cinnamon).

choo: latrine, toilet.

CMS: Church Missionary Society.

debe: a four gallon kerosene tin; empty tins used for carrying water, food storage, and (flattened) for roofing of houses.

dudu: insect.

duka: shop.

furaha: joy, happiness.

gadamoji (Borana): tribal coming of age ceremony.

hodi: 'May I come in?' (called out by visitor at the door).

karibu: 'Come in!' or 'Welcome!' (response to *'Hodi'*).

kikapu: woven, grass shopping basket.

kiroboto: flea.

kuku: chicken.

lugga (Borana): dry river bed, gulley.

mabati: corrugated iron

mandasi: cakes (usually deep-fried doughnuts).

mugumu: wild fig tree:

mwananchi: lit. 'a son of the land', a native.

mzee: an old man; title of respect.

Mzungu: European, a white person.

NFD: Northern Frontier District.

ndio: yes.

NIV: New International Version of the Bible.

NRSV: New Revised Standard Version of the Bible.

panga: machete.

sana: very.

shamba: garden, small-holding.

siafu: safari or soldier ants.

sufuria: saucepan.

tackie: plimsoll, gym shoe.

tamu: sweet (adjective).

ugali: a thick porridge made from maize meal.

woya (Borana): man's white robe.

CHAPTER ONE

It was the soap that gave me away. The required items list, sent to my parents by Nairobi Primary School before the start of my first term, included two bars of toilet soap. These were then taken into custody by the dormitory matron at the beginning of term, and pooled for communal use. Each day, after games, came bath time. We were herded into the dormitory bathroom, clambering two by two into the steaming hot, but increasingly murky, water. Matron stood by, exhorting us to remember to wash our ears and to scrub our muddy knees. It was a happy interlude in the day, a fun time, without demands. We shouted, sang lustily to the echoing walls, and spread water far and wide on the bathroom floor. And, for me, it was an introduction to luxuries of which I had, so far in my life, been unaware. Lux, Palmolive, Pear's Coal Tar – they were new names to me, new smells, new smoothness. And I luxuriated in them. Until one day a howl of protest rose above the normal cacophony of the bathroom. *'Who* brought this stuff?' And there, lying in all its glory on the ledge of the bath, was one of my two rough-cut blocks of bright red Houseboy carbolic soap. It was what we always used at home. Houseboy was a product of Kenya's Elephant Soap Factory. In fact they made no fewer than two brands of soap – red for personal use, and yellow for laundry. It came in long waxy bars, which could be chopped up into blocks. It was utilitarian and it was cheap. And that had been my contribution to the communal ablutions of my dormitory – two hunks of the Elephant Soap Factory's very best red Houseboy soap. But I had to confess, alongside the neatly wrapped, sweetly scented, skin-friendly imported soaps that the other boys had brought, mine was very obviously different.

My soap was different because I was different – or so I felt. I was a *mishkid*. My dormitory mates were the sons of settler farmers, of government officials and business men, of teachers and other professionals. But I was a mishkid – the son of missionaries. It put me in another category. True there was one other mishkid in the dormitory. George, the son of Presbyterian missionaries at Tumutumu, north of Nairobi, was older than me – he was seven, I was six. But George had three advantages over me – his parents lived near enough to Nairobi to take him home on leave-out Sundays; and they had a Model-T Ford with a dickey seat at the back; and George's parents gave him respectable soap. I had none of these advantages. My parents lived three hundred and sixty very rough miles away; and they drove an old, ex-army Dodge Battlewaggon; and they gave me Houseboy soap.

But the advantages of growing up a mishkid in colonial Kenya far outweighed any disadvantages. Those years of my childhood in Kenya, from my birth in 1941 until my departure to study medicine in England in 1958, were, for the likes of me, privileged years indeed. Though we were slow to realise it, we were living in the twilight of Empire. Racial segregation; separate schools for Europeans, Asians and Africans; the assumption of white supremacy; the colonial mentality – all were in their last throes. The recently ended World War had ushered in a new world. The winds of change were blowing. And my generation experienced the first gusts of change, the last stand of empire.

My generation of white Kenya kids represented several very different communities. The children of civil servants, and other government employees, were often relative newcomers to Kenya. Their parents had been posted to the colony. They sometimes arrived at school fresh from England, with very white skins, rosy cheeks and relatively long shorts. We called them, disparagingly, *pongos*. They soon tanned and toughened up, and took inches off their shorts. Their parents, the colonial officials of the day, are usually regarded nowadays with disapproval, even contempt. They are accused of exploitation and arrogance. The truth is that many of the white government officials of the time carried out their jobs with exemplary dedication and expertise. Many indigenous

Kenyans who recall those colonial days remark on the lack of corruption, and the ability to get a fair hearing and a just ruling. Some of the white provincial and district commissioners, and young district officers, were men of great ability and integrity, and do not deserve to be tarred with the racist, exploitative brush.

Another category of my school contemporaries was that of sons of settlers. Some were the offspring of British parents, some of Boers who had trekked up to Kenya from the Cape earlier in the century. Most of the boys in this category were Kenya born, and in many cases their parents were also Kenya born. They felt and believed themselves to be *wananchi* – 'people of the land'. They had, by sweat and blisters, hacked their farms out of the bush. They had suffered sickness and setbacks, privation and loneliness. Yet they could not imagine living anywhere else. They had invested their lives in Kenya, and they loved the country passionately. They belonged to it, and it belonged to them. Except that it didn't! Perhaps because of their paradoxical situation – having the land but not being of the land – they felt somewhat threatened and vulnerable. This caused some (but not all) to be arrogant and aggressive in their attitude towards Africans. They understood African culture and spoke the local languages better than most, and yet they were often the least ready to mix socially with Africans. Boys of South African Boer origin tended to be the most racist. Perhaps they felt that they had already been displaced once, from South Africa, and they were not prepared to be displaced again. It was a *laager* mentality. The coming years would differentiate painfully between those who were prepared to adapt to an independent Kenya, and those who were not.

Then there were us mishkids. In a school of five or six hundred pupils we probably numbered about thirty. Our background differed from that of other boys in several respects. Unlike the sons of some Government officials and businessmen we were in Kenya for the long haul. Most of us had been born in Kenya. Our parents had had what was, in those days, normal for missionaries – a life-long call to missionary service. Not for them the short-term tour of present day missionaries. Not for them the modern 'hit-and-run' approach, whereby no sooner have you begun to master the language, and to understand the local culture, and to build bridges of friendship, than your two year term of service is over. Not for them the hassle of temporary work permits. They went overseas for life. They sold any property they had in their home country, and with all their worldly goods packed into crates and tin trunks, they said their goodbyes and sailed for the land of their calling. It was total commitment. Many raised their families overseas, and many died overseas. And so, by dint of our parents' vocation, we were born in a far-off land.

In that respect we resembled the sons of settlers. We were children of the land. But the reason for our parents being there differed very much from that of the settlers. Settlers had staked a claim on the land. They were there, in their opinion, for keeps. Their land would become their children's land. And whether it was by growing coffee or cattle, sisal or sorghum, pyrethrum or pineapples, their farms were their investment and their source of income. Their lives were invested in the very soil. By contrast the missionaries were not there for what they could get, but for what they could give. They did not, personally, own any land. They were often posted, during the course of a lifetime, from one mission station to another. Some were preachers, some teachers; some were doctors or nurses; some agriculturalists or engineers; some were experts in linguistics, and devoted themselves to translation of the Bible. They devoted their lives to what they considered to be a God-given calling. If asked where exactly in the world they *belonged* they would probably have replied in the words of the writer to the Hebrews:

> For here we have no lasting city,
> but we are looking for the city that is to come.
> *Hebrews 13:14 (NRSV)*

They were pilgrims, and happy to be so. But for us mishkids this posed a problem. We knew no other country. We knew no other life. We belonged to Kenya. We belonged by birth and upbringing. We heard our parents speak affectionately of England, the *home country*. But we did not know England, and when in due course we came here, we did not at first like England. We did not like its culture and its crowds. We did not like its clouded, smoky skies. We grew up as children of sunshine and bare feet, children of the wide open spaces and freedom to roam. We were children of Africa, wananchi. Kenya was in our blood. And yet we did not belong there, because our parents did not belong. They were on a pilgrimage, and we had happened to join them. They knew where they were going – to serve God in Kenya for life. But did that make us children Kenyans? Had God called us to Kenya too? Was this calling genetic? Or did we really belong back in that distant and strange land from which our parents had been called?

Where in the world we belonged was a problem and a confusion that we each had to resolve for ourselves. It would seem that, on the whole, those children whose parents returned them to the homeland before their teens had less problem settling into life in the west. But those who stayed on in Kenya for their secondary schooling, as my brother Dennis, sister Marilyn, and I did, had a much greater problem adjusting to life in Britain. Quite a number of us mishkids returned in due course to East Africa as missionaries ourselves. Others found secular employment in the land of their birth, and stayed on there, or returned after further training in Britain. Some eventually settled in countries such as Australia or New Zealand, which have a sunny, outdoor lifestyle, more akin to Africa than to Britain.

'Mishkid' was actually not a term that we used at the time. It was probably an Americanism that crept into the vocabulary at a later date. But it was a useful description of the likes of me. Mishkids are now no longer called such. More sophisticated terms replace old simplistic ones. They are now called TCKs (Trans-Cultural Kids), which includes a wider range of children than just those of missionaries. The new term indicates that the problem has been recognised. Missionary children (and others) are brought up in a foreign culture and environment to which they do not belong, but to which they want to belong, and which causes them intense nostalgia when eventually they are removed from it. I write as one who has no regrets whatsoever about my parents' calling, and its repercussions on my life. There are of course other mishkids who bitterly resent their parents calling, often because of the separation from parents that was entailed, and the traumatic experience of being sent away to some distant boarding school.

Whether a mishkid's, or TCK's, childhood experience was a happy one, or a traumatic one, inevitably the cultural ambiguity left its mark on us. We have a choice. We can regard ourselves as children of no-man's-land, born by chance of circumstance into a culture to which we did not belong. Or we can consider ourselves children of exceptional privilege, whose birth into a far-off land was all part of God's plan. We experienced the richness of having parents who had little materially, but whose faith and dedication was an example and an inspiration. We grew up with Africans as our friends, and the vast open spaces of Kenya as our playground. It was my deep privilege, through God's grace, to be a mishkid, and, for my childhood at least, to be a true *mwananchi,* a son of the land.

CHAPTER TWO

My life began in June 1941 not far from the Ngong Hills, that range of blue, rolling hills to the west of Nairobi, made famous by Karen Blixen: 'I had a farm in Africa, at the foot of the Ngong Hills.' So begins her evocative book *Out of Africa*.

Our little stone bungalow, called Mushroom Hall because it sprang up almost overnight, was at Dagoretti Corner. This was where the road out of Nairobi forked – right to the green uplands of Kabete; left to the Ngong Hills and Karen, the area named after Karen Blixen, and where she had lived. It was to Dagoretti Corner and to Mushroom Hall that my mother, Ruby, brought me back, a bundle in a shawl, from the Eskertine Nursing Home. Eric, my father, was on compassionate leave from the war. A chaplain in the King's African Rifles, he was at the time serving in Ethiopia. The war had interrupted my parents' missionary work at Marsabit, in Kenya's remote Northern Frontier District. We – Eric, Ruby, my two-year-old brother Dennis, and now me – were a family temporarily displaced.

My earliest memories are of Mushroom Hall. The little verandah was crammed with lush vegetation – ferns, begonias, geraniums, fuchsias growing in profusion in green-painted *debes*. Plants always grew for Mum. She and they seemed to have an understanding. She could turn a stark verandah into an oasis. She could create a flower bed in a desert. I remember the neat, low christthorn hedges which lined our drive, with their sharp prickles, and milky sap, and brooches of orange-red flowers. I recall the peach tree which, when in fruit, was festooned with brown

My mother, Ruby Webster, and father, Eric Webster.

paper bags, each protecting a peach from the predations of mousebirds. Part of the garden at Mushroom Hall consisted of a grove of eucalyptus trees, with their long dark green leaves and peeling, curling bark. I can smell now the acrid smoke of burning eucalyptus leaves, swept off the drive by the gardener. Behind the bungalow was a small hillock, crowned by a large *mugumu* tree. It was on this knoll, in the cool shade of the tree, that I was put each afternoon for my siesta. By the age of two I had graduated from a cot to a camp bed. I discovered one day a hole in my pillow. With some skilful attention I was able to enlarge the hole sufficiently for it to emit a very satisfactory shower of feathers whenever I threw the pillow into the air. Fluffy white down, drifting in the hot afternoon air, was enough to keep a small boy amused for some time.

My earliest unpleasant memory was of *siafu*, or safari ants – those fierce soldier ants which march in relentless columns, eating anything that gets in their way. It was a day when Mum had a visitor, and they were engrossed in rather dull conversation. So I rode my tricycle to the entrance of our drive, and peered over the culvert into the ditch below. And there was a winding, bustling, seemingly endless column of *siafu* on the march. The large soldier ants bridged the column protectively, their fierce jaws touching across the procession, while the hordes of workers scurried beneath their arch. I had never seen a sight like this before. I leaned further to get a closer view. And further. And then, in a flash, my tricycle had tipped, and I fell head first into the ditch, right onto the column of *siafu*. In a moment I was smothered by furious ants, their large pincers slicing into my flesh. They were in my clothes, in my ears, my mouth, everywhere, nipping, burning. I felt on fire. I fought to disentangle myself from my tricycle, and I ran screaming to the house, where Mum and her elegant lady visitor furiously plucked ants off me. Soon they too were smothered, and the visitor had to retire to the bedroom to shed some clothing. It was some time before we were all ant-free.

World War Two did not altogether by-pass Kenya. There had been the threat of invasion by the Italian army from occupied Ethiopia. Sea passage to the homeland was almost impossible, and imports from Britain had dwindled to nothing – making Kenya of necessity much more self-reliant. Our toys, as young children, were wooden ones, crafted locally. Many men, both from the white and black communities, were recruited into the army, mainly into the King's African Rifles. Having, together with South African troops, repelled the threat of invasion by Italian forces to the north, and having expelled the Italians from Ethiopia, the King's African Rifles moved on to Madagascar, and then to Ceylon and Burma. For many African soldiers, fighting this white man's war, the whole experience was an eye-opener to a wider world, and to new possibilities. The soldiers' women folk meanwhile continued to raise their families back in Kenya.

Mum, once settled into Mushroom Hall, got employment as a teacher at nearby Kilimani Primary School. It was a school for white children. From time to time we ventured into Nairobi, in her little green Austin Seven, to shop. Nairobi had not yet been granted the status of a city, but it had all the airs and graces of a capital town. Delamere Avenue, named after the father of the colony, Lord Delamere, was broad, and boasted date palms and bright shrubberies of bougainvillea and golden shower and blue plumbago. There were glass-fronted shops, two hotels and a statue of Lord Delamere in the middle of Nairobi's only roundabout. Government Road, leading down to Nairobi Station, was the other main shopping street. Its single storey buildings, with their corrugated iron roofs, and porticos shading the pavements from the hot sun, boasted every kind of shop that a white citizen might require. The days of traffic jams had not yet arrived. Nor the days of traffic lights. (When the first traffic lights were installed in the 1950s an African was arrested for cycling through a red light. When asked by the magistrate if he understood the rules about traffic lights the accused replied, *'Ndio Bwana!* When the light is green all the Europeans go. When it is yellow all the Asians go. And when it is red we Africans can go.') The dusty box body cars of settlers from upcountry vied with donkey carts, and with rickshaws conveying white memsahibs about their weekly shopping trip. Always there was dust, and noise, and smells, and an air of excitement. The highlight of the trip, for us, was an ice cream in the cool of a café.

Better for us, though, than the elegant shops of Delamere Avenue and Government Road was Bazaar Street. This was the Indian quarter of Nairobi, and this was where bartering was to be done, and bargains to be had. The shops were open-fronted, their contents spilling on to the pavement. There was a heady mix of blaring Indian music, and exotic odours of spices and joss sticks, and open sacks of rice, and bales of colourful cloth, and tailors with tape measures in hand eager to size you up, and others busily peddling at their street-side Singer sewing machines. And long bars of red and yellow Houseboy soap from the Elephant Soap Factory. We ran the gauntlet of polite but persuasive shopkeepers: 'Please step inside *memsahib!*'; 'Yes, *memsahib!* How can I help you? Whatever you need we will get! We are getting next week!'; 'Madam, this way please!'

At the end of Bazaar Street was Nairobi Municipal Market, a seemingly vast building, with fruit and vegetable and fish stalls downstairs, and curio stalls around the upper balcony. Here the urgency and the eagerness of stall holders to sell was even greater than in Bazaar Street. Voices echoed around the high building. The smell of exotic fruit and fish and carved wooden souvenirs mingled. Vendors were persistent: *'Tamu sana, memsahib!* Very sweet! You try!' And with that they would slice into an orange or, even better, a mango, and hand you a segment, dripping with juice. Soon our *kikapu* would be bulging with luscious tropical fruit. This, to me, was Nairobi proper. This was Africa.

There were occasional reminders that we were a country at war, though my own recollections of them are faint. A detachment of the King's African Rifles, perhaps on their way to war, or back on leave, might march by under the command of their British officer. With their caps and neck flaps, and shining bandoliers, and khaki uniforms and puttees, and rifles aslope, and a swagger in their step, they were proud to be soldiers of 'Kingi George'. On one occasion, when the Italian invasion was still a threat, and I was just a babe in a pram, our shopping trip was broken by an air raid warning. Everyone took cover in narrow side streets or shops. But no bombing raid ever came – perhaps it was just a practice. Dennis became the proud owner of a cap badge, donated by a soldier who took refuge in the same side street.

I have dim memories of a holiday at Malindi, on the Kenya coast, with Mum and Auntie Edith. Malindi is now the Blackpool of Kenya, with hotel after hotel lining the beach. Then it was unspoiled – miles of empty beach with just one hotel, the Sinbad, and a scattering of very basic palm thatched, self-catering cottages. We stayed in one such, owned by a Mrs Sunde. The breakers pounded the shore in front of the cottage. The *makuti* thatch rustled in the on-shore breeze. Colourful geckos shimmied up the cool white distempered walls of the banda. A whole bunch of sweet, yellow 'ladies' fingers' bananas hung in the eaves of the verandah. Fishermen brought fresh fish and lobsters to the door. It was paradise. Not such a pleasant memory was a trip to the Blue Lagoon, at Watamu. There I was knocked over by a large wave,

David and Dennis at Malindi with Auntie Edith.

and disappeared under the water. Fortunately my parents noticed my disappearance, and hauled me to safety. I have memories of lying under a coconut palm, coughing up sea water. A fear of water remained with me for some years afterwards.

The day came when I was old enough to start at Mrs Watts' Nursery School, in a valley just down the road from Kilimani Primary School. Equipped with my little lunch case, and my obligatory pith helmet, or topi, to protect my head from the supposedly dangerous tropical sun, I ventured into the world of education. I regret that I very soon disgraced myself. I threw sand into the eyes of a little girl who had annoyed me, and was made to stand, shame-faced, until playtime was over. It was a lesson which remains with me to the present time – it is not good to throw sand into the eyes of a girl. Dennis meanwhile had moved on to the giddy heights of Kilimani School, where he was taught by our mother.

Dad, by now a Major, and a senior army chaplain, had occasional home leave. He brought with him various khaki-uniformed 'uncles' – mainly soldiers from Britain, far from their own homes, with nowhere to go on leave. I began to learn, from a very early age, the joy of an open, hospitable home. We had living with us at Mushroom Hall, for part of the war, Dad's sister Edith. She was a missionary in Samburu, two hundred miles north of Nairobi. Missionary colleagues of hers, Charles and Jessie Scudder, had two small children, Godfrey and John. Godfrey had had a very traumatic birth at a mission hospital, and had sustained severe brain damage. He needed a lot of extra care. Tragically Charles Scudder was diagnosed with cancer soon after the onset of war. To return

Padre Webster in his army chaplain uniform.

to Britain for treatment was impossible. Instead he and Jessie went to South Africa, leaving Godfrey and John in the care of Mum and Edith at Mushroom Hall. During this time both Scudder children had critical illnesses, and it was thought at one point that both might die. Mum and Edith carried a heavy responsibility. Charles and Jessie Scudder returned from South Africa when I was a few months old. Charles had seemed to have responded well to radiotherapy, but within a few days of his return he suddenly relapsed and died. Jessie later lost Godfrey too, but then served the rest of her life as a missionary in Samburu, bringing up John, one of my fellow mishkids.

Once his regiment went off to Ceylon and Burma, Dad could not return to Kenya on leave. It was not until Hiroshima and Nagasaki brought the war in the east to an end, on 14th August, 1945, that the East Africa contingent began to return home. Mum prepared us for his coming. I was too young to remember him, but sensed the rising excitement. So the day came when we stood on the platform of Nairobi Station as the troop train from Mombasa pulled in, hissing and panting after its six thousand foot climb from the coast. And suddenly there he was, my father, just one of hundreds of men, black and white, each dressed in khaki, each seeking out, on the crowded platform, the familiar faces of their loved ones. In spite of all the preparatory excitement, I found it hard to accept that this uniformed stranger, who drove us home to Mushroom Hall, was my father. Leaning forwards I whispered confidentially in my mother's ear, 'Who that man who come in chuff-chuff?' The war over, we could begin, for the first time since my birth, to be a proper family.

CHAPTER THREE

Mum and Dad, and all the other missionaries whose work had been disrupted by the war, began to make plans to return to their mission stations. There was also the matter of home leave to Britain. It was ten years since Dad had last been home, and Mum had not been back since she sailed to marry Dad in 1937. Nothing could happen immediately however. Dad had to be demobbed. Mum had to work out her notice at Kilimani Primary School. There were very long waiting lists for sea passages back to Britain. The priority for Mum and Dad was to make a short visit to Marsabit, to see how the Christians were faring. They were greatly encouraged. The young church had grown in numbers, under the leadership of an Ethiopian Christian, a refugee, Stephen Dere. Dad found a number awaiting baptism. The mud and thatch church had been rebuilt and enlarged (still in mud and thatch) for the princely sum of £25 – a considerable amount in those days, and raised entirely by the Marsabit Christians. The absence of missionaries had encouraged them to take responsibility, and to grow as an indigenous church, without looking to missionaries for leadership and money.

It was not until towards the end of 1946 that we obtained berths on the *SS Cameronia*.

Building the new church.

She had been converted to a troop ship. Thousands of soldiers were anxious to get home. Others, like us, were Kenya residents due for home leave. This was going to be no cruise trip. Women and children were packed into the cabins, two families per cabin. All men slept in hammocks in dormitory type accommodation. The Red Sea, Suez Canal and Mediterranean had not yet been cleared of mines. We had regular lifeboat drill. On two occasions it was for real – mines had been sighted in our path, and we had to make sudden alterations in course to avoid them. We finally docked at Genoa. It was night, and we found ourselves next to the *Queen Mary,* also commandeered as a troop ship. To a five-year-old the Cameronia seemed large, but, in comparison, the *Queen Mary* was vast. I remember looking up and up in awe at the lights of her port holes.

We docked at Tilbury to find a Britain bruised and battered by war; people exhausted by years of struggle and privation. The rubble of bomb sites had yet to be cleared. There were shortages of many commodities, and food rationing was in full force. It was a tired, grey, drab Britain, and yet a Britain relieved to be at peace once again, and determined to rebuild, its people hanging on by sheer stubbornness and grit. Of course these were not my thoughts or perceptions at the time – I was far too young to understand post-war Britain. But it explains things that I do remember. I remember the stark skeletons of bombed buildings. I remember that sweets were a weekly treat, and I remember the skill with which my grandfather could slice a soft-boiled egg in two, and up-end it before the yolk spilled. Half an egg a week was our ration. I don't know how our grandparents managed to feed us all. The privations of post-war life passed us children by.

We made our way north to Thornton Cleveleys, near Blackpool, to a semi-detached, pebble-dash house in Hillylaid Road – the home of the Webster grandparents, Caleb and Gertie. It was a house bulging at the seams, because we arrived at a time of great significance. Dad's elder brother, Harold, and wife Edie, were home from their missionary work in the Arctic. With them were their two daughters – Ann (an adopted daughter, whose Innuit mother had died) and Marguerite. This was Dennis' and my first experience of cousins. Also there was Aunt Edith, back on leave from Kenya. And the youngest sister of the family, my Aunt Ella, home from Liverpool. A nurse, she was about to marry a jocular young pharmacist, Don Wilson. This was to be the only time, after Harold, Eric and Edith set out on their missionary ventures, that the family would all meet together. Where we all slept I have no idea – I think we were farmed out to friends and neighbours. That precious two weeks of reunion was a riotous time. Grandma Webster, with her long, flowing white hair pinned up in a coil, bustled happily about the house, her mutterings to herself interspersed with snatches of Moody and Sanky hymns. I liked Grandma Webster – she was warm and cuddly. Grandpa, with his prominent Roman nose on which perched his round wire glasses, and with his studious air, was more austere.

Grandpa and Grandma Webster.

Uncle Harold, was a replica of my father, though a few sizes larger. He had the bulbous Webster nose, and the Webster wit. On Sunday we all went to the local parish church for morning worship. I found myself sitting in the pew between Dad and Uncle Harold. As a five-year-old does before a service, I was browsing through the prayer book, and came to the Table of Affinity. 'A man may not marry –' it declared, and then proceeded to say whom a man may not marry. First on the list was '– his grandmother'. This was a puzzle. If grandmas were warm and cuddly, as mine was, why should marriage to them be forbidden? I turned to my father and whispered, 'Daddy! Why can't a man marry his grandmother?'

'Shhh! I'll tell you after.'

A nudge came from the other side. It was Uncle Harold. 'Go on! You ask him!'

I repeated, more loudly, 'Daddy, why can't a man marry his grandmother?'

'Shhh! Not now! I'll tell you later.'

Another nudge. 'Go on! Ask him!'

So, loudly now – loudly enough for the reverent congregation to hear – 'Daddy, why can't a man marry his grandmother?'

Heads turned. Sniggers were stifled. My father turned red. And Uncle Harold, later to become Archdeacon of the Arctic, looked quietly pleased. To this day I have not been told why a man cannot marry his grandmother. Uncle Harold was rather special – but then, for a long time, I thought he shared a name with God, a fact I was reminded of whenever I recited the prayer 'Our Father who art in heaven, Harold be thy name …'

The gathering of the Webster clans over those two weeks was not just fortuitous. It was for Ella and Don's wedding. This was the only wedding of their offspring that the Webster parents attended. Harold had been married to Edie on board the annual supply ship to Aklavik, in the Arctic. The ship brought the bride with all the accoutrements for a wedding, and the ship's captain, who was licensed to do so, conducted the ceremony. He then sailed away, leaving the happy couple to an Arctic honeymoon. There had been no family or friends at all at their wedding. Eric and Ruby had been married in Nairobi, just two days after Ruby's arrival by sea. She was given away by someone she had met only two days before. Edith never married. It was not for want of opportunity. An eligible young clergyman had proposed to her most earnestly, but she had to choose between him and her calling to be a missionary in Kenya. The calling won the day. So Ella's wedding was a very special and unique occasion for Caleb and Gertrude. Marguerite, Ella's eight-year-old niece, was an obvious choice for bridesmaid. But what about a page boy? Ella suggested me, but on the strong recommendation of my parents I was turned down in favour of brother Dennis. I was apparently liable to phases of total non-cooperation, which could occur at any time during the ceremony. I was thus spared the indignity of dressing up in ridiculous satin garb – or so I chose to regard my rejection!

During the ensuing twelve months of leave we made further visits to Thornton Cleveleys. Blackpool sands did not quite live up to the wild stretches of glistening white sand, and the thunder of breakers on the coral reef, and the rustling coconut palms, of Kenya's seaside. But there were compensations – donkey rides, and the big dipper, and ice cream cones and Blackpool rock. Old black and white photographs show Dennis and me, our bodies vested in knitted swimming suits, digging in the muddy sand, while grandparents – Grandma in full dress and smart hat, and Grandpa in suit and tie – sit proudly overseeing us from their deck chairs.

It was at our other grandparents, my mother's parents, Grandma and Grandpa Bloor, that we spent more of our leave. Grandpa Bloor had retired at the end of the war from his work as a foundry foreman in Derby. They bought a three-storey terraced house at 11 Hartington Street, with a view to letting out two of the floors. For the duration of our leave we occupied the middle floor. It was a base, somewhere to settle a while and to enjoy family life. Missionaries on home leave so often have to live a nomadic existence, sharing the homes of tolerant parents or friends, but with little opportunity to be together as a family. At Hartington Street we had our space. Dennis and I were enrolled at nearby Reginald Street School, myself in the nursery department. But nursery or not, it was where I met my first girlfriend. She was a snotty-nosed, freckled, little thing, whose name I forget. But my ardour was sufficient to make me walk on the grass in the park where the notices said 'Keep off the grass', in order to pick daisies for her.

Winter came harshly that year – 1946/47. It was the winter of winters, the Big Freeze. It began to snow on 23rd January, and it continued to snow and freeze until 17th March. Day after day thick snow lay on the ground, with new pristine layers added. In many parts of the country snowdrifts fifteen to twenty feet deep brought traffic and industry to a standstill. Frozen pipes, power cuts, electricity rationing, empty

Grandpa and Grandma Bloor
outside Alpine Cottage.

shelves in shops, crippled public transport and unemployment added to an already miserable existence for many people. In our small world in Derby the gardens and hedges of Hartington Street disappeared under feet of snow. The acrid smell of burning coal fires filled the air. The traffic stopped. Sledges appeared. For Dennis and me it was of course a new and thrilling experience. The drab street was turned into a magical world of white. When the snow first fell I insisted on carrying a handful home for Grandma – and discovered for the first time the agony of frozen hands. Dennis and I made snowmen, and hurled snowballs, and skipped through the powdery white wonderland, oblivious of the hardships many were experiencing.

Another new encounter was with prevalent infectious diseases. We both caught mumps and measles, and we were very ill. I remember being delirious, with confused and terrifying dreams. The yellow wall paper of our bedroom seemed to contort and distort, to advance and retreat, and I cried out in my delirium. Finally the fever broke and the worst was over. Meanwhile Grandma and Grandpa Bloor had let out their ground floor flat, and had bought a cottage, Alpine Cottage, in the Derbyshire village of Bonsall, high in the hills above Cromford. Here we could go to convalesce. But there was no escaping the harsh winter – in Bonsall the snow lay even more thickly than in Derby. Dennis and I slept in a loft, up a ladder. Each morning we came down to a new adventure. Fresh falls of snow in the night would have piled against the front door of the cottage, and Grandpa had to dig through it. The cottage was situated on a steep, winding lane, the perfect site for hair-raising sledge rides. And Grandpa Bloor was the perfect person to take small boys on hair-raising sledge rides. With shrieks and shouts and arms raised aloft, Grandpa in the driving seat of the sledge, and one or both of us perched in front of him, we would career down the hill and round the steep bends before finally crashing into a snow bank at the bottom of the hill.

Grandpa Bloor was fun. Blinded in one eye as a youth by a handful of lime which was thrown at him, he also had a scar on his nose from an air gun pellet, which narrowly missed his other eye. He was bald-headed and jolly. He and Grandma came from a very strict 'closed' Plymouth Brethren background, but they had broken free from that (had, in truth, been excommunicated for attending a Pentecostal service), and became part of a much more open and friendly Assembly. We loved him and his tricks and jokes. We also loved Grandma Bloor, who was quiet and adoringly tolerant of her mischievous husband.

At last the long, harsh winter ended. The banks of snow melted, and as they turned to water so the floods rose. Roads turned into rivers. Rivers turned into torrents. A wonderland of snow became a flood land. Then spring broke through – myriads of daffodils nodding enthusiastically at the warm sun; fields of cowslips and banks of primroses. Derbyshire burst into new life. The wooded slopes that flanked the Via Gelia were carpeted, wall to wall, with bluebells, their delicate scent filling the air. We picnicked in the fields around Bonsall, and romped on the rich grass and clover, clambering over our long-suffering Grandpa. He took us on expeditions in his black Austin car – his pride and joy. We went to Dovedale, and dared one another over the famous stepping stones. We watched dippers diving for food in the clear, tumbling waters of the River Dove. An exploration of Dovedale's caves was turned by Grandpa into a Great Adventure. We climbed Thorpe Cloud and skimmered down the scree slopes. The caverns of the High Peak district offered even greater adventures. Speedwell Cavern, a flooded Roman lead mine, was explored by boat, propelled by a guide lying on his back and 'walking' along the low, rocky ceiling. At intervals he lit candles, placed in brackets on the walls of the cavern – so leaving a trail of flickering lights, reflecting on the water. All these were the memories that lingered in my impressionable mind, and were the things that I remembered about England throughout my childhood.

Eventually that seemingly endless leave came to an end. Kenya was calling us back. For my parents it was God's call, a call that took priority over all other considerations, whether of family or finance. And as children we were inevitably part and parcel of their call. The goodbyes of our parents to their parents were painful. Who could tell when, or indeed whether, they would meet again? (In fact my mother would not see her mother again.) We sailed from the Royal Albert Docks in London, on the Llangibby Castle, on 24th July, 1947. The sea voyage was, in those days of slow travel, in itself an antidote to culture shock. There was time to adjust. The ship called at Marseilles, Genoa, Port Said, Port Sudan and Aden – each a place with its own interests and excitements. At Port Said and Port Sudan 'Fuzzy Wuzzy' traders swarmed out in their boats, to cluster around the ship, like ants round a sugar lump. Bartering and trading was conducted by shouts, and the feverish raising and lowering of baskets of goods from the busy little boats to the ship's decks. Days at sea were given to gentler pursuits – deck quoits, reading and dozing, and for us children, exploration of the ship. There was time on board to make new friends. A large number of passengers were Christians, mainly missionaries returning to their places of work after leave, or heading for the 'mission field' for the first time. Dad started a daily Bible Study group, to which thirty-three came. After a month at sea the palm fringed shores of Mombasa came into view, and the ship edged its way through the reef, and entered the deep waters of Kilindini Harbour. It was 23rd August. For the first time since their marriage in 1937 Eric and Ruby could look forward to returning to Marsabit, and to taking up their work again, without the threat or the actuality of war. They could also look forward to us being a family – in our own home.

CHAPTER FOUR

The journey from Nairobi to Marsabit was a daunting one. It was a distance of three hundred and sixty miles, of which only the first fourteen, to Ruiru, were tarmacked. After that mud, potholes, dust, sand, riverbeds, rocks and corrugations could be expected – in generous amounts. A sturdy vehicle was necessary. Fortuitously some ex-army vehicles were on the market, and Dad acquired, on behalf of the mission, a four-wheel-drive Dodge station wagon. It was robust. It had a powerful (and thirsty) engine. It was roomy. And it was extremely uncomfortable. Any form of suspension had presumably been considered a luxury incompatible with warfare, and had been omitted. We set out for Marsabit from Mushroom Hall, the Dodge packed to capacity, both inside and on the roof rack, with our luggage and supplies. This was just the first of many such journeys to and from Marsabit in the years to come. Dad was an expert packer. In BCMS (Bible Churchmen's Missionary Society)

Eric and the Dodge at Isiolo.

circles it was reckoned that he could fit more into a vehicle than any other missionary. On one later occasion, following a BCMS conference, an admiring group of fellow missionaries watched in wonder, outside the Church Missionary Society (CMS) guest house in Nairobi, as the pile on the roof rack rose skywards. With loud acclaim we set forth on our journey, and travelled just twenty yards, to the bougainvillea archway at the entrance to the guest house, where we came to an abrupt halt – the arch was only fractionally higher than the roof of the Dodge. Everything had to come off, and then be reloaded out in the road. Eric's reputation for packing took a dive that day.

On this journey however there were no obstructions. Dennis and I settled into the nooks which Dad had made for us amongst the luggage. We were in high spirits. When Dad was in high spirits he sang, and today he sang. Soon we were through the outskirts of Nairobi, and were passing the coffee plantations and pineapple estates of Thika. Then, pursued by a thick cloud of red dust, we were into the green, fertile, cultivated hills of the Kikuyu Reserve: Sagana; Karatina; Fort Hall. Groves of banana trees and plots of maize clung to the hillsides. Kikuyu women, festooned with beads and bangles, were bent double as they hoed the red earth, their babies sleeping peacefully on their backs. We passed women laden with enormous bundles of firewood or sugar cane, and others carrying *debes* full of water, balanced on their heads. Children waved cheerily as we passed, and shouted *'Mzungu! Mzungu!'*

As we neared Nanyuki, one hundred and twenty miles north of Nairobi, on the western slopes of Mount Kenya, the landscape changed. We were entering white settler/farmer territory. The green hills and red, foaming rivers gave way to the grassy plains and black cotton soil of cattle and sheep ranches and wheat fields, sprawling up the slopes of the mountain to the forest edge. The air was much colder, as a bitter wind blew down off the glaciers of Mount Kenya. We stopped at Nanyuki for a picnic break on the banks of the icy Nanyuki river. It was also the chance to refuel, and to buy any supplies that we had forgotten. And so on again, over the shoulder of the mountain to the Ngare Ndare escarpment. Here the road plunged sharply down, zig-zagging its way to the hot plains north of mount Kenya. A vista opened up before us – the legendary Northern Frontier District (always known as the NFD). As far as the eye could see, fading into

The barrier, entrance to the NFD.

the distant blue haze, ranges of jagged mountains rose sharply from the thorn-tree plains. Ol Lolokwe, Wamba, Warages, Ol Donyo Lengeyo, the Matthews Range, the Ndoto mountains. Somewhere beyond them, and not yet visible in the haze, was Marsabit mountain, our home-to-be.

We were now into hot, dry thorn bush country. There was an occasional homestead, but no signs of agriculture. Herd boys grazed cattle and goats in the scrub. The soil was rocky and sandy. In just fifty miles we had passed from lush, glacier cooled forest to semi-desert. We entered the straggly frontier town of Isiolo. A wide dusty road ran between two lines of shabby corrugated iron *dukas*. There were administrative offices, a police post, a prison, a post office, a dispensary, and some houses dispersed in the bush. This was the 'capital' of the NFD. We stopped at one of the *dukas* to refuel – both the Dodge and also ourselves, with cool drinks – before the final one hundred and seventy mile stretch to Marsabit. Nobody set out on the next stretch without first calling at the Post Office to see if there were letters for Marsabit. There might not be another vehicle for days. And so we came to the barrier, the entrance to the NFD. A permit to enter was required, and a book had to be signed, with details of the vehicle, the passengers, the reason for the journey, and, most important, the time of entering the NFD. If one did not turn up at the other end at least someone would know for how long one had been missing. The *askari* raised the barrier and waved us through. We were on the last leg home.

This was the most challenging leg by far. The heat of the day was over, and within another two hours nightfall would suddenly descend. We needed to find a suitable place to camp. Twenty miles north of Isiolo we crossed the Uaso Nyiro river – the only permanently flowing river in the NFD. Rising in the Sukuta plateau, and disappearing at its termination into the Lorian Swamp, the course of the Uaso Nyiro can be traced across the plains by the green ribbon of doum palms which line its crocodile infested, muddy banks. The Marsabit road crossed the river at Archer's Post, by a concrete bridge – only the width of one vehicle, but nevertheless a proper bridge. Nowadays vanloads of tourists turn off here for the Samburu Game Park. Then there was just wilderness. The red earth road curved and headed towards the sheer rocky mass of Ol Lolokwe. Dad knew of a spreading thorn tree at the roadside, near the base of Ol Lolokwe, and there we would spend the night.

It was indeed a good place to camp. A spreading acacia tree, festooned with weaver bird nests. A breeze to keep the mosquitoes at bay. Plenty of dead wood for the camp fire. Flat rocks to sit on. Bushes to disappear behind for personal matters. A magnificent view of the rock

Ol Lolokwe.

Weaver bird nests in an acacia tree.

face of the mountain. It was a connoisseur's camp site. There was also an abundance of wildlife around – dikdik, gerenuk, giraffe, zebra, even elephants. It was the latter that caused us to keep a camp fire burning all night. Dennis and I eagerly gathered dead wood for the camp fire, keeping a wary eye out for snakes and scorpions. We ate our supper, a can of baked beans heated by Mum in a *sufuria,* around the sparking fire, feeling content and warm and safe within our circle of glowing light. Dad recounted to us tales of his travels in the past, of days when he travelled by foot with camels, to take the Good News to the desert peoples around Marsabit. He read the day's portion from Daily Light, and we commended our journey to God. The red embers of the fire and the chill night air reminded us that it was time for bed. Another long day lay ahead. We put up our camp beds at the side of the car, and lay for a while gazing up at the jet black, scintillating night sky. Finally – to the sound of a hyena's howl, the sharp bark of a jackal, the eerie crack of a branch as something moved in the bushes – finally sleep overtook us. It was the first of many future magical nights camping in the NFD.

The dawn chorus woke us. The weaver birds in the tree above us set up a cacophony of twittering. Red and yellow barbets called to one another, their calls perfectly synchronised and sounding as one. A black and white turaco shouted its raucous 'Go away!' from the top of an acacia. The air vibrated with the sounds of awakening life. The orange orb of the sun rose rapidly above the thorn tree horizon, and before we had finished our breakfast the heat of the day was beginning to reflect off the ground. It was time to re-pack the car and continue our journey.

The monotony of the road, the heat, the dust, the jarring vibrations from the corrugations, were broken by the frequent sighting of animals. It became a competition as to who could spot them first. We were driving through a paradise of wildlife – herds of elephant, reticulated giraffe, grevy zebra, black rhinoceros, warthogs, Grant's and Thompson's gazelles, gerenuk and dikdik, ostrich and secretary birds. The list was endless. It was a time when the land was very sparsely populated, poaching was rare, hunting was restricted, and the wildlife was unmolested. We kept a tally of what animals we saw, and how many. We also, to help pass the journey, claimed a mountain each, and we would look out for 'our' mountain. I claimed Ol Lolokwe. Dennis selected a mountain in the Ndoto range that was marked by a deep cleft. He named it *'Panga* (machete) cut'. Dry river beds also helped to mark our passage. There were eleven in all that we had to cross between Isiolo and Marsabit – seasonal rivers running off the mountain ranges to the west. Some had rickety wooden bridges, comprising planks laid crossways on wooden beams. We rattled horribly over those. At other riverbeds the bridges were either unsafe or non-existent. At these we had to drive down onto the soft sand and, with four wheel drive and engine revving, plough our way through. Great cheers from us and a snatch of song from Dad marked our safe passage.

Half way from Isiolo to Marsabit we crossed the widest of the seasonal river beds, the Merrille. Forty miles on was the watering hole of Laisamis, on the edge of the Kaisut Desert. Rendille herdsmen, in their finery of mudded, ochred hair and beads, and with spears in hand, were supervising the watering of their camel herds. The sun beat down mercilessly on the rocky, treeless landscape. Now the site of a Catholic mission and hospital, the only building then was an open sided shelter

The Merrille river bed.

which afforded a patch of shade for the Government Livestock Officer when conducting the occasional purchasing of camels and goats for market. It was on a future occasion, when Dad was bringing to Marsabit his newly appointed secretary, Gwen Kerr, who had just arrived in Kenya from Ireland, that he told her on the journey that they would be accommodated that evening at the Laisamis Hotel, and that formal dress would be expected. Gwen was very concerned that she had nothing smart with her, and Dad expressed doubt as to her acceptability at the hotel. Truth, of course, dawned when they arrived at Laisamis, and

Gwen burst into peals of Irish laughter at her gullibility. She had come to work for a joker and a tease.

The landscape now changed from barren to even more barren, as we entered the Kaisut Desert. Vegetation was scraggy and very sparse. Spiralling dust devils snaked

Shelter at Laisamis.

and writhed into the air, as they raced across the hot sand, vacuuming up debris from the ground, flinging it round and round in their vortex. Outcrops of blistering black lava rock rose here and there like warty growths on the desert face. But on the horizon beyond we could now see the smudgy blue outline of Marsabit mountain. Home was in sight. The road deteriorated to a deeply rutted track. Fine dust billowed behind the vehicle, and rose up into it through every possible aperture, coating us with a ghostly deposit. Midway across the desert was the rocky bed of the seasonal River Milgis. We passengers walked, while Dad eased the Dodge over the hundred yard stretch of boulders which formed the dry river bed. A few more miles and we came to Logologo, or, as we called it then, Lugga Loho – a dry gulley, or *lugga,* which marked the base of Marsabit mountain. We began to climb. We were on the home straight. Long grass grew up the middle of the track. The landscape became greener, lusher. Above and ahead was grey-green forest, clothing the top of the mountain. Soon we were skirting the forest edge. Many of the trees were festooned with lichen, 'old man's beard'.

We passed a water hole, Ulanula, the 'Place of Leeches', where a herd of cattle were being tended by Borana tribesman in white *woyas,* and their womenfolk in skins. At intervals down the well hole were wet, slippery cross poles, set into the mud sides of the well. And balanced on each pole stood a man or woman, passing a steady and relentless flow of skin water vessels up and down to one another – vessels full of muddy brown water up, to be emptied into the cattle trough; empty vessels down to be refilled. It was a seamless circular motion, born on the tide of a haunting, rhythmic chant, which rose from

Watering the cattle.

39

the depths of the well, and the very depths of their souls. Water and cattle – this was the very stuff of life; this was the heart of their existence. We passed Ulanula. Occasional roadside homesteads began to appear. We were approaching civilisation. Before we reached the township of Marsabit we turned off and up a very rough, rutted track which brought us, one lurching mile later, to a clearing on the edge of the forest. We had arrived at Karantina, the site of the mission. Dad and Mum had come home, to the place where they believed God had called them. And we had come too.

The mission at Karantina.

CHAPTER FIVE

We knew when we had arrived at the mission compound because an avenue of windswept jacaranda trees marked the drive. Our home was built from stones hewn from a rock face in the forest, and the house backed right on to the forest edge. The other missionary house, a smaller, wooden building, festooned in golden shower creeper, was where my parents had begun their married life ten years previously. But this was no longer big enough for our expanded family. It became the

The stone house, before the verandah was added.

home of Barbara Gibbins, the mission nurse. The two houses had been commandeered by the army during the war, and used as sick quarters. In fact Dad had at one point during the Ethiopian campaign been admitted as a patient to his own bedroom. Now, once again, they were to become homes. We had a living room, with fireplace, and two bedrooms. At the back was an echoey bathroom containing just a zinc bath. There was no running water, so no taps and no flush toilet. The kitchen contained a Dover stove, heated with firewood from the forest. There was a larder, containing a meshed food safe – the meshing to keep flies out, but to allow a cooling breeze to blow over the home-made butter, the milk and the meat. There was no such convenience as a fridge. Meat came from the butcher in the township. It was nondescript. He sold us whatever he happened to have. It might be a hunk of cow, sheep, goat or even camel. Every week it included a large, wobbling sheep's tail, which would be rendered down to fat balls, used for cooking.

Lighting was with kerosene pressure lamps and Dietz lamps. Along the front of the house ran a verandah, overlooking the mission compound. We could see who was coming and going. Large, black, wood-boring wasps had riddled the posts of the verandah. A painful sting taught me never again to stick a finger into the holes. Down one side of the house, and running into the forest edge, was a path leading to the long-drop, the latrine, the *choo*. It was possible to perch on the wooden seat of the *choo* and watch baboons disporting themselves in the nearby forest trees. They in turn could watch with equal fascination humans doing their business in the latrine. A visit to the long-drop, far from being a chore, was often quite an adventure. In order to save others a wasted journey anybody going to the latrine hung a rope across the path to indicate occupation.

My parents' return to Marsabit was the cause of great excitement among the local populace. Employees of the mission lived mostly in a row of mud houses along the jacaranda avenue – 'the Lines'. The rest of the local community lived in scattered homesteads, set among their maize and banana plots, on the hillside opposite the mission. Soon a steady stream of welcomers was converging on the stone house. 'Mirta' (the 'Runner', as Dad was nicknamed because of his tendency to run everywhere) and his family were back. There was so much to tell, so

Some of the first Christians.

many questions to ask, such a lot of time to catch up on. Dad and Mum were most anxious to hear news from the Christians. Were they standing firm in their faith? Who had come to faith? What was the state of the Church? And there was much to encourage them.

Dennis and I were much more intent on investigating our new home. The mission compound was ten acres in extent, which gave us plenty of scope for safe exploration. Much as we would have liked to explore the forest that would not have been safe on our own – there were elephant and buffalo in abundance. The other buildings on the compound comprised a stone dispensary, a wooden school building (Mum's domain), a mud walled office (Dad's domain), and the open sided, mud and thatch church. The dispensary attracted me from a very early age. It always smelt strongly of antiseptic, and dettol was probably the chief medicament used by the nurse, Barbara Gibbins. Certainly her pharmacy was basic, and the medical procedures she could offer were limited.

The dispensary.

But what she could and did offer in abundance was care and time, and she was loved for that. She spent many a night sitting with a mother in labour, or at the bedside of a critically ill child. Each day groups of patients would congregate on the grass outside the dispensary to have their wounds and fevered brows tended by 'Sisista' Barbara.

The wooden school building had, in the 1930s, been the home of Wesley Haylett, a pharmacist sent to Marsabit in lieu of a doctor. He came with his wife, who gave birth to their first child, but then became ill with pneumonia and died. The four roomed building was now Marsabit's first and only school – a primary school, with standards one to four. The pupils in Standard One varied in age from six to sixty, and their keenness to learn to read and write was palpable. Mum was an inspired and dedicated teacher, and she oversaw the early education of some of Kenya's future leaders.

Dad's mud office was really the nerve-centre of the work of the mission. Here he would spend many hours each day, in discussion with individuals, bashing out letters on his old Remington typewriter, preparing talks, and ensconced with local Christians in translation of the Bible. Not only was he responsible for the running of the Marsabit mission. He was also Field Secretary responsible for all the BCMS missions across East Africa. It was a big responsibility, and involved much paper work as well as safaris of thousands of miles. It meant that, even in school holidays, we often did not see as much of our Dad as we might have wished – though he did his utmost to remedy this.

The church building was of mud walls and thatch, with a mud floor. The seats were timber benches, rough-hewn from the forest. One side wall was only waist high, and gave a panoramic view down a forest-clad valley to the foothills of the mountain, and the desert beyond. The church bell consisted of a piece of railway line suspended in a tree. It was struck by another piece of metal, and as the clanging rang out each Sunday, and echoed down the valley, so people began to emerge in their colourful Sunday best from their scattered homes on the hillside, and to wind their way along a network of paths to church. Dad, standing up front in his clerical robes, would announce the first hymn – often the Boran translation of a song from *Golden Bells* or Sankey's *Sacred Songs and Solos*. As Mum pedalled furiously at the little harmonium, the strains of the hymn would be taken up by the packed congregation with more gusto than melody, and would ripple down the valley. For Dennis and me the open side of the church was a saving grace. We were expected to attend church each Sunday morning, and yet the services were both long and, to us, incomprehensible, being in Borana. So it was not long until our attention strayed from the service to the forest. Here we might see a pack of baboons, playing and quarrelling noisily in the canopy. It was when they fell silent that we knew they were up to no good. They learned that the church bell signalled an opportunity to raid our garden while we were otherwise occupied. The echoing first hymn signalled the time to move in. On many a Sunday they crept up on our vegetable plot, and pawpaw and banana trees, and wreaked havoc while we were at worship.

Three reminders of the past intrigued me. One was the wild fig tree under which Dad, Charles Scudder and Alfred Buxton had pitched their tent when they first arrived in Marsabit in 1931. I used to try to imagine how it had been in those early days. White strangers in a remote land, knowing no local language, having no means of communication other than by gestures and smiles. The question uppermost in the minds of the

Eric and Charles Scudder under the wild fig tree.

Eric's first house, made of grass.

local people must have been, 'Who are they, and why have they come?' Another relic of the past was a circular cement patch, overgrown with a profusion of purple bougainvillea. This was the remains, the floor, of my Aunt Edith's mud and thatch house, which had burnt to the ground many years before. That was before Mum joined Dad in Marsabit, and before Edith moved to Maralal. I used to try to imagine what her house had been like, and how helpless she must have felt when her home and all the possessions she had in the world went up in flames. But Edith and Eric and Ruby, and their missionary colleagues, did not put much store by possessions. The third reminder of the past Dennis and I discovered in our explorations. Just inside the forest edge was a small enclosure surrounded by a high thorny kei apple hedge. Within the enclosure was a grave stone. This is where Wesley Haylett's wife had been laid to rest, a symbol of the ultimate sacrifice that a missionary could make. The hedge was to protect the grave from wild animals. It had grown wild, and the grave was uncared for, forgotten. This made me sad. I did not know Mrs Haylett – she died long before I was born. But her widower and child were not there to care for her grave. So I took it on myself, from time to time, to place a few flowers on the stone.

Our house being so close to the forest edge, we often had elephant or buffalo in the garden at night. Mum and Dad would wake us, and I remember watching spell-bound from the living room window, as the

Blind Daudi Dadacha.

vast, shadowy shapes of elephants moved silently past the house. We could hear the rumbling of their stomachs, and the crack as they tore branches off trees. Or it might be a herd of buffalo munching on the lawn, sinister and blacker than night, their massive bosses and horns eerily silhouetted against the moonlight. On occasion elephants ventured close to the house even in broad daylight, browsing on the forest edge.

Dennis and I were soon revelling in our new home and playground. We roamed free and barefoot. Soon the soles of our feet became hardened to the stones and thorns that abounded. Each night, around the pressure lamp, Dad would check our toes for jiggers, and as often as not dig one or two out with a safety pin. We began to make lasting friendships with our African contemporaries, and a group of us became playmates. Elisha was the son of Daniel Godana, one of the first converts to be baptised in Marsabit. His home lay just outside the mission entrance. Luka was the son of Daudi Dadacha. Daudi had been blind from early childhood. He too was an early convert to Christianity, and he felt a calling from God to share the Gospel far and wide. During the course of his life this blind evangelist walked thousands of miles over hills and deserts, led with a stick by a relative or friend. Until young Luka enrolled at Marsabit school his chief occupation had been to lead his father. Daniel and Solomon were the sons of Daudi Danabo. Again he was one of the very first Christians in Marsabit, and had shown great promise as a future leader in the church. Tragically he had died young, and Daniel and Solomon were brought up by their uncle, Phillipo Mato. Mattayo was the son of Yonah and Loho. Andarea's father had been killed in his *shamba* by a marauding elephant – crushed to death. Gedde was the son of Chirqo, who had only half a nose. Part had been bitten off, it was said, by his wife, in a spat. Elisha, Luka, Daniel, Solomon, Mattayo, Andarea, Gedde and others became our childhood friends. They all went to Mum's school, and this strong foundation of schooling led, in due course of time, and with further schooling elsewhere, to them all becoming influential in independent Kenya.

But all that lay far into the future, and little would we have dreamt it possible at the time. Dennis and I too needed an education. He was now eight and I was six. As white children in colonial Kenya the path of our education was destined to differ from that of our African friends. For us it would be boarding school in far away Nairobi. And it was to Nairobi Primary School that our attention now had to turn.

CHAPTER SIX

The journey southwards, and schoolwards, was much less exciting than our journey up to Marsabit had been. Boarding school itself was a new adventure, but it was the leaving home and parents that I dreaded. We had packed our school trunks, with regulation school shirts and shorts and ties, with favourite books and precious toys – my best dinky car, my small green teddy. Things a six-year-old was going to need. And, of course, bars of Houseboy soap. We drove as far as Nanyuki, the railhead. We booked in to the Sportsman's Arms Hotel, a very colonial institution, inhabited by a rather eccentric group of long-stay white residents. Accommodation was in individual cottages, each with a sitting room and log fire, to ward off the chill mountain air. But such pleasures were not for Dennis and me. We were destined to board the Nairobi train at 10PM. It would then remain in a siding until 6AM, when it would depart on the six hour journey to Nairobi. Dennis and I washed and changed into our pyjamas at the hotel, and then Dad and Mum took us to the station at the appointed hour. The strange mixture of excitement and dread became entangled, and formed a knot in my stomach. Already there was a gathering of other children at the train. The boys looked so big and so confident. So tough. There was a teacher present to escort us, but the four-bunk compartments had no connecting corridor, so the amount of supervision was going to be limited. Our tin trunks were stowed in the luggage van. We were allocated our compartment and bunks, were introduced to our compartment companions, who were instructed by the teacher to 'look after' us, and the awful goodbye moment arrived. Mum later wrote to her parents, 'We tucked the boys up in their bunks for the night, and came away feeling terribly sad and lonely. They looked so young and small to be leaving home.' They, and we, were paying part of the price of a missionary calling – separation, often at an early age.

I was awoken by a loud whistle followed by a sudden jolt. It was pitch dark. We were moving. The train protested with squeals and groans as we slowly gathered speed. The engine panted faster and louder, and the wheels responded with a rhythmic clackety-clack. I thought of my parents back at the hotel, and how with every clack of the wheels the distance between us was lengthening. Soon we were all fully awake. Up went the blinds, and the mosquito netting shutters. The excitement of the journey took our minds off the parting. The train belched its way through fertile valleys, sometimes almost doubling back on itself. We halted at little stations, where hawkers on the platform sold sticks of sugar cane and mugs of hot, sweet *chai* with *mandasi*. Naro Moru, Nyeri, Sagana, Karatina, Maragua, Thika. The stations marked our passage, further and further from home. At times, as we crawled up inclines, people hitched lifts, clinging precariously to the outside of the train. We saw little of our escort teacher – just a quick head at our window when we stopped at a station. Eventually the hills gave way to flat sisal estates, their serried, spiky ranks stretching to the horizon. The scruffy suburbs of Nairobi appeared, and finally the bustling, echoing station. Our teacher took on a new air of urgency and efficiency and command, marshalling us into a semblance of order, checking that we had donned our uniforms correctly, supervising the loading of our trunks onto the school lorry. No longer were we individuals. We had become part of a system, elements of an institution, cogs (small ones at that) in a machine. We were at school.

Nairobi Primary School was in a commanding position on a hill overlooking Nairobi. There were three boarding blocks, east, west and central, each of two storeys and built around a central quadrangle. These accommodated about five hundred boarders, both boys and girls, and all white. The main school building was an impressive structure with a central bell tower and hall, and two wings of classrooms. Most of the classrooms however were temporary wooden structures, on stilts. My

Front steps and pillared hall, Nairobi Primary School.

destination, on that first day, was Junior dormitory, on the top floor of west block. And here I met my dorm matron, Ma E, a lady in her twenties, sporting a flashy engagement ring. She was the one to whom my welfare, and that of nineteen other six and seven years olds, was committed. If we had hoped for kindness and warmth, a mother substitute, we were to be disappointed. Ma E was a sadist, who seemed to delight in discipline and punishment. She soon laid down the rules – bedside lockers at all times to be tidy and subject to random inspection; beds to be stripped and remade tidily each morning, with hospital corners; mosquito nets to be coiled and tied in a neat knot above each bed. There was to be no crying, no night-time sobbing under the blankets. Home-sickness was for sissies. Any bed-wetting would be announced and the culprit humiliated before the dormitory. No talking after lights out. And so on. Most of these heinous crimes would be punished with the *tackie* – a beating on the bottom with a plimsoll.

I broke the rules on that first night, and on many nights to come. Burying myself under the coarse school blankets to stifle my sobs, I pined for home. On many a night I stood gazing from the toilet window, which had a grandstand view of Nairobi. Far below I could hear the plaintive, haunting whistle of trains at the station. They spoke of the way home, and of freedom. I broke another rule unwittingly. One night I was woken by a boy climbing into my bed – he was sleepwalking. I prodded and pushed him, but he just snuggled down into my bed, still fast asleep. All I could do was to move over and make room for him. And there he remained until morning, when Ma E found us in this, to her, compromising position. She seemed to forget that he was just seven years old, and I was six. We were both thrashed with the *tackie* for such outrageous behaviour.

Our housemaster was no more congenial than Ma E. Known irreverently as 'Bucksarse', he carried a permanent scowl, and a permanent drooping cigarette. He seemed to have an innate dislike of mishkids in particular, and for some reason known only to himself he soon nicknamed me 'Daniel'. I certainly felt that I had entered a lion's den. I had the feeling that he regarded me as a 'goody-goody', and was waiting to catch me out. His opportunity came. I had gained confidence, and (as small boys do) looked for opportunities to impress and amuse my dorm mates. I had always been taught by my parents not to swear, but in the school environment this was seen as a sign of weakness. But I found a compromise solution, which I recited to the impressed dormitory after lights-out one night: 'The ruddy butcher threw the bloody meat over the dam wall under the blinking stars, and it landed among the blooming flowers.'

But, unbeknown to me, Bucksarse was listening just outside the dormitory. 'Webster! I'll deal with you tomorrow!' he yelled. And so next morning at breakfast, in front of the whole boarding house, I was hauled up by Bucksarse and accused of swearing in a most offensive way. I got 'six of the best' on my bottom, there and then in the dining room.

Saturday mornings began with letter writing time. We all had to write home, and to present the unsealed letters for approval of both content and tidiness by the supervising teacher. This censorship made it difficult to say too much to our anxious parents, and we usually put a brave and positive face on things. But one of my early letters did get through the system uncensored. I was feeling very homesick and sad, and was crying as I wrote. Large tears fell onto the page, blotching the ink. Lest my parents missed their significance, I actually labelled the blotches 'These are tears'. I don't know for whom the separation was hardest – them or us.

But there was one ray of light in our boarding block. It was Ma Simpy. She was the tiny, white-haired catering matron, and she had a huge heart of love. Each night, after Little Boys' Supper, she would line us up, and give each of us a hug and a goodnight kiss. That one gesture of love, that moment of friendly physical contact, was a treasured moment in the day. Perhaps Ma E and Bucksarse had personal, domestic problems. Perhaps they had been badly treated themselves in childhood. Perhaps they enjoyed too much their positions of power. For whatever reason they made those early days at boarding school particularly unhappy for a home-loving, sensitive, little six-year-old. Ma Simpy helped to redeem the situation.

So did some of our class teachers. My form teacher, in Standard One, was Ma Moody. She was pretty and she was kind. I loved her and worked hard for her. Not generally loved was Ma Murdy. She taught music, but had the handicap of a permanently hoarse voice following some surgical accident. This caused her great frustration when she was trying to teach us to sing – she would burst into attempted song, but all that emerged was a croak. Likewise when she became angry with us, and attempted to shout. All that emerged was a hoarse whisper. This frustration, and the stifled sniggers it caused, would make her even more angry. But behind her fiery temper lay a very kindly person, and I was fortunate to experience that side of her. She was one of the best teachers I had.

Organised sports were never my forte, and perhaps one reason for that lay with our games teacher. She lined us up on the touch line and then walked down the row, inspecting our physique. She picked out for the football team those who met her physical standards. When she came to me she told me that my legs were the wrong shape for football, and I was rejected. I never did discover what shape one's legs should be for football, but it was a rejection – and a complex – which stuck with me for the rest of my childhood. I was not good at football (or hockey or rugby or cricket) because I was the wrong shape. It was an inevitability.

Three Sundays a term were leave-out Sundays when pupils were free to go out for the day. That was fine for those who lived near Nairobi, or whose parents came 'down country' in order to take them out. But for Dennis and me this was not a possibility. However friends came to our rescue. George's parents were Presbyterian missionaries at Tumutumu, in Kikuyu country. So George, like Dennis and me, was a mishkid. His parents were sympathetic to us, and would sometimes take us to their home. They had a Model-T Ford, with a dickie seat. Here we boys would proudly sit, our hair blowing wildly, red dust billowing around us, as we sped to Tumutumu. It was on such a leave-out, on a straight stretch of road, that for the first time in my experience we reached the incredible speed of sixty mph. On very special occasions Dad was able to organise mission meetings in Nairobi to coincide with our leave-out. How I looked forward to those occasions, but the goodbyes at the end of the day were very traumatic.

Although at times I hated boarding school, although I so missed my parents, and longed for the holidays, I would not have had it any other way. Would I have preferred my parents to have had some other job, better paid, more generally respectable? No! I was proud that they were missionaries, doing what they were doing. Would I have preferred them to have lived somewhere more central and civilised, where perhaps I could have lived at home, or at least seen them regularly, as other boys saw their parents? No! There was nowhere in the world that I would have chosen to live more than in Marsabit. For all the hardships and separations entailed we were content. I was glad to be a part of my parent's missionary call. Nevertheless, I longed for, I counted the days off until, the end of each term, and that happy, magical day when our trunks appeared in the dormitory for re-packing, and we sang lustily in school assembly 'Lord dismiss us with Thy blessing. Thanks for mercies past received', and the Dodge appeared at the school entrance, and we were going home.

CHAPTER SEVEN

It is not everyone whose father builds their house, let alone builds it out of mud and poles. But that is what Dad did. Marsabit had long needed a doctor, and the Mission had tried without success to recruit one. Before the war they had sent a doctor-substitute in the form of the pharmacist, Wesley Haylett. But he had left when his wife died postnatally, leaving him with a baby to care for. They then sent Dr Reginald Bunny, but his time was cut short by the war, and the evacuation of Marsabit in the face of an impending Italian invasion. And he had been there long enough to discover that the Marsabit mists did not suit his asthma. After the war he remained as the doctor in Naivasha, in the Rift Valley, with its hotter, drier climate. For ten years Marsabit had had no doctor, apart from the occasional visits of a Government Medical Officer from down-country. Now, at last, a doctor was coming – Dr Jo Taylor and his wife Joan. They would need a house, and the obvious one was the stone house, our house. So Dad set to build us a new house. It would be sited near the church, at the head of the valley that overlooked the far desert. Poles were cut from the forest, and also thin, pliant *fito* – saplings

The Webster family home, built by Eric.

fastened crosswise to the upright poles, and between which mud was packed. Dennis and I helped the mission workmen to tread the red mud, which oozed and squelched between our bare toes, and then fell with a satisfying flump between the fito. The walls rose. As they dried they were coated with a thin layer of cement and painted with distemper. Stones quarried in the forest were hammered and crushed to build up the floor. The roof trusses were trees from the forest, and they were clad with *mabati* – corrugated iron, second hand and already riddled with nail holes. Not surprisingly it was later found to leak in many places, and the cement floor was marked with crosses at those places that required strategically placed buckets. For ceilings we had rolls of papyrus matting, bought at the roadside in Kikuyu country.

We loved our new house. It had a cool, damp smell to it, and a homeliness. The sitting room sported a polished green cement floor, and some basic furnishings, including a bristly elephant-foot stool – the relic of an elephant which had killed a man just near the mission. Although Dennis and I had a bedroom in the house, we preferred to spend our holidays in the separate guest rondavel, with its high thatched roof and view down the valley. The kitchen was also a separate building at the back, equipped with a smoky Dover stove, fuelled with firewood from the forest. Its detachment from the house was a blessing, not only because of the smoke from the stove, but also because of the odours from the *kuku* pan. '*Kukus*', in East African terminology, are chickens, and Mum kept chickens. Every bit of waste food went in to the *kuku* pan, which simmered constantly on the stove, like a witches brew. Even dead moles and mice went in to the *kuku* pan, and, at the end of the day, the noxious brew was mixed with laying meal and fed to the hens. Nothing was wasted. Even the entrails, head and feet of a slaughtered hen would be recycled. I am convinced that sometimes our eggs had very dubious flavours.

As at the stone house, so with the new house the toilet was a long-drop, a choo. It lay down a windy path beyond the avocado pear and custard apple trees, and before the banana grove. As with most African long-drops, it became home to a variety of spiders, beetles, hornets, even (occasionally) a snake. 'Going to the toilet' was no routine chore but an adventure, especially at night, when elephant and buffalo were about.

The Webster children in the rose garden.

Mum had green fingers. She was a passionate gardener, and it was not long before the house was surrounded by beds of canna lilies, streptosolon, verbena, gaillardias, bougainvillea, even roses – all thriving in the rich red volcanic soil. She had been informed in her early days in Marsabit, by a self-opinionated Government official, that it would be impossible to grow temperate fruit in Marsabit, particularly apples. So Mum grew apples. And custard apples, naartjies, limes, grenadillas, golden passion fruit, pawpaws and bananas. A vegetable patch soon appeared, surrounded by a buck and elephant-proof fence. Maize, potatoes, beans, peas, carrots, tomatoes – soon all were growing in abundance, and we were self-reliant in fruit and vegetables. But it was not easy. There were constant attacks from above and below – from above by marauding packs of baboons, who leapt over the fence at church time, and stripped the garden in minutes. From below by crawling locusts, called *aderashas,* which fed voraciously on tender plants. Mum's defence against these consisted of empty food cans, with tops and bottoms cut out, placed over every seedling in the vegetable plot. A cursory glance at our garden might have led a visitor to think that we were growing serried ranks of cans of spaghetti and baked beans.

The upkeep of the garden, the chopping of firewood, the cooking on the temperamental stove, were all time-consuming occupations. And Mum and Dad, with their church and mission duties and a school to run, did not have a lot of time. So the success of these domestic enterprises depended very much on African staff. To employ a cook and a gardener was not feudal but practical. Besides, it provided needy people with an income. Our gardener for many years was Dube. Short, stocky, grizzle-headed, quietly spoken, Dube would appear through the morning mist, his *woya* wrapped around him and knotted over his shoulder, to discuss the day's work with Mum. He developed a passion for gardening and skills that matched those of Mum. They were a formidable duo, co-conspiritors, and on many a misty morning in the school holidays could be seen digging together, or conferring over the latest strategy to defeat baboons and *aderashas*.

For a while Petro Oce was the cook. Tall, dignified, serious, he would survey the pans on the stove with an air of haughty disdain – as though their contents were slightly offensive, their speed of cooking unacceptable. Peering through his steamed up round glasses he would prod them into obedience. A skill that Petro learned was to make ginger biscuits. It was a much appreciated skill, until the day when he mistook the tin of pepper for that of ginger, and set our mouths on fire. In due course Petro went in to the ministry, the first local person to be ordained, and he took to surveying his congregations in much the same way as he had surveyed his pots and pans. Our friends, Elisha and Luka, Daniel and Solomon, needed to earn school fees. And to work for us from time to time, in school holidays, was a way of helping them. But it led at times to a rather confusing relationship. On the one hand they were our friends, almost part of our family. Eric and Ruby called them 'son', and they

Elisha, Solomon and Daniel.   Musa and Luka.

called Mum and Dad 'mother' and 'father'. But when they did holiday jobs for us they became employees, and were not free to play with us. So what were they – servants or chums? I think – I hope – that over the years it was the friend-relationship that proved lasting. To our white fellow schoolboys it seemed incredible that we had African friends, who played with us, and ate with us, and were called 'sons'. Perhaps more than anything else this differentiated us from others at school. It was all part of being a mishkid.

We had to create our own amusements in the holidays – no television, of course, but not even radio. A little portable Robert's radio, with an aerial slung into the trees, and powered by a car battery, caught crackly, barely decipherable snatches of news once a day, and we would gather round in silence, ears glued to it. But there was no question of listening to it for entertainment. We had a wind-up HMV gramophone, and a small selection of Bakelite records – *The Colonel Bogey March; Sandy Powell; the Messiah.* It was not a great choice for young boys, but we made do. Colonel Bogey was useful when we played soldiers. With the aid of Dad's war time officer's caps, and with home-made sashes, we and our friends marched around the mission compound. We built our own mud hut, our 'military headquarters'. The game often ended in a dispute as to whether Dennis or I was the more senior officer. Our friends were content to be privates. We played dinkies and constructed Meccano. We played church – Dennis always the preacher, I the congregation (which is perhaps why he ended up preaching, and I practising!) We built a tree house, and we made a raft out of oil drums to float on a dam in the forest. Each holiday we produced a play or a conjuring show. All our games involved imagination and invention. They were not served up on a ready-made plate, in the way that computer games are served.

An exciting gift one Christmas was a large white box kite, ideally suited to Marsabit's strong winds. It soared up and up until it was way above the hill that separated the mission from the township. And then a trickle of breathless people began to arrive from the other side of the hill. A white object had appeared in the sky. The rumour spread. It was the moon, come down over the mission – and they came to see. It must have been disappointing to discover that the moon was attached by a string to a small white boy.

We had bicycles, which we used mainly around the mission compound. But sometimes we ventured to the township – perhaps to the *dukas,* to buy sugar for Mum; or to the telegraph office to send a telegram for Dad; or possibly to visit the house of a government official. The police inspector at Marsabit, in our early days, was Keith Cowen, and he had a son and two daughters, a bit younger than us. His wife, Diana, was an avid stamp-collector, and she helped and enthused us in the hobby. It is no coincidence that Dennis (many years later of course) married the elder daughter, Priscilla Cowen. The district commissioner, 'Windy' Wild, had no less than five daughters, but at that age they had little appeal to us as playmates – we much preferred our African friends. I suspect we barefoot mishkids had even less appeal to the Wild girls.

We became owners of horses almost by default. A departing official persuaded Mum and Dad to take on their much-loved horse, Brigadier. In due course he was joined by two Abyssinian ponies. It must have been a sociological challenge for Brigadier. He was aristocratic, pure-bred, trained. The ponies were coarse, ignorant vagrants in comparison. One of them always refused to allow a rider to mount from the side, and would kick and bite if anyone so tried. The only safe way to mount him was to drop onto his back from a tree – the 'mounting by surprise' technique. One reason for acquiring the ponies was to facilitate out-reach safaris to

David on a part-trained Abyssinian pony.

Boran villages on the lower slopes of the mountain. It was also thought that they would help the nurse, Barbara Gibbins, with visits to outlying patients. Barbara's horse-riding career was brief. A passing donkey, laden with empty kerosene tins, was startled by the horse, and shied, causing a loud clattering of the tins. The horse consequently bolted. Barbara tried to leap from the horse's back, but her foot caught in the small Abyssinian stirrup, and she was dragged through the bushes by one leg. She survived, though bruised and battered. It was her first and last attempt at riding. Dad then bought her a motorised bicycle. She practised down the mission drive. She was supposed to stop at the mission entrance, but instead continued out through the gate, gathering speed. She entered a dip, and disappeared from view. She did not reappear, but a sickening thump was heard from Daniel Godana's banana grove. Barbara had discovered a way to stop, but not the recommended one. Her moped career ended. After that she always used a bicycle. But because the road from the mission was rough and steep she always pushed it downhill. And, on return, and for the same reasons, she always pushed it uphill. But at least that way she never fell off, and the carrier of the bicycle accommodated her medicine case.

Holidays passed all too quickly. Once past the half way mark I would feel a growing sense of dread. Mum and Dad would try to cheer us, 'We shall be down for one of your leave-outs this term!'

Response: 'What about the other leave-outs?'

Or: 'You've got that nice new teacher this term!'

Response: 'All teachers are nice to parents; she'll be horrid to us!'

Or: 'It's cricket this term. You enjoy cricket!'

Response: 'Legs are the wrong shape for cricket!'

Trying to cheer us up was a lost cause. But there came the occasion when Dad said, 'I've got a surprise for you. I'll tell you about it when we are on the journey.'

'I expect it's some chocolate or something!' we responded gloomily.

'You wait and see,' he said.

CHAPTER EIGHT

We said our tearful goodbyes to Mum, and were on our way to school, the car not as full for a downward journey as it would be for the return one. 'So what's the surprise then? Where's the chocolate?' we asked Dad.

He looked slightly bashful. 'It's better than chocolate! You are going to have a baby brother or sister!'

That news certainly was better than chocolate. For some time now we had been praying for a sibling, but not simply for a brother or sister. We wanted, specifically, a sister. The previous year Mum had been expecting a baby. But then one day the runner from the telegraph office had arrived at the house with a telegram. Mum's mother, Grandma Bloor, had died. It was not entirely unexpected – cancer had been diagnosed a few months previously. Mum had known for a few weeks. But there was no question of returning to England. The trip would have taken many weeks, and the cost was anyway beyond their means. There was not even any quick way to communicate – no telephone, no airmail. Of course no texting, no skype. The news came in a stark telegram, just a few words heavy with grief. Mum took the telegram away from the house to a quiet place down by the kei apple hedge, where she could weep alone. But I followed her, and we wept together. That last goodbye, the previous year, had indeed been final. She could not even be there when her mother was laid to rest in the churchyard on the hillside in Bonsall.

Grief followed on grief. Soon after that Mum had a miscarriage. A long hoped and prayed for baby was lost. But now she was going to have another – a girl, if prayer had any efficacy at all. It was a few months later when Mum was found to have an abdominal swelling that was not part of the pregnancy. It was a rapidly growing ovarian cyst. She was admitted to hospital in Nairobi, just along the road from our school. Dennis and I were allowed out of school to visit her. My teacher asked me why she was in hospital, and I told her with confidence that she was having 'a sister removed'. 'Cyst' and 'sister' had become confused in my mind. However the cyst went, and the sister survived. The baby was due during the August holidays, and we were loaned a small cottage at Limuru, in the green highlands twenty miles from Nairobi. On our way in to Nairobi, for Mum's last check-up before the birth, the steering rod of the car snapped. We veered off the road, mounted a bank, and were deflected back across the road, narrowly missing a lorry that had been following us. We came to rest in a cloud of dust, shaken and shocked. Dennis (the one of us who later went in to the church, not medicine) asked hopefully, 'If the baby had been a boy, could that fright have changed it into a girl?' If it was, then it did. Because Marilyn joined our family a few days later, sporting a mop of dark hair. Dennis and I were proud indeed.

David and Dennis: proud brothers with their sister Marilyn.

That was by no means the end of Mum's medical problems. While Marilyn was still breast feeding Mum was diagnosed with breast cancer. At the time it all passed us by – we were too young to understand the implications. She had what was then the only treatment on offer – a mastectomy. Marilyn as a toddler invented a game – she would peer down the front of Mum's dress, and exclaim 'Only one!' Mum joined in the spirit of the game, and they would both convulse with laughter. Neither then, nor at any time in the years to come, when the cancer returned, did Mum ever show any sign of self-pity. Her only wish was to live for the family's sake.

The Webster family complete.

Dad too had a medical adventure, but his was self-imposed. He had long worried that if, when away on safari, or even in Marsabit itself, he were to develop appendicitis there would be no quick access to surgery. Mum had had her appendix out together with the ovarian cyst. Now Dad decided to have his out as a preventive measure. He was admitted to Nairobi Hospital. He had with him things he had bought for Marsabit, including a plastic potty for baby Marilyn. This became known in the ward as 'the padre's tea cup'. For Dennis and me our parent's respective admissions to hospital were a bonus. They were held captive in hospital just along the road from school, and we had unexpected opportunities to see them during term time.

My vocation to medicine arose out of one of Mum's hospital admissions. We were told on that occasion that children would not be allowed to visit. It occurred to me that if I became a doctor I would be a member of the establishment, a part of the system, and therefore able in the future to visit her, and to take her grapes, at any time of any day. This seemed the best of all reasons to become a doctor. I remember telling her of my intentions, and she was grateful. And so, in due course, this is what I did. Perhaps because of my intended career I was called on at a very early age to exercise surgical skills in the dormitory. A boy had, at some time in the past, been accidentally shot in the cheek by a friend with an air gun. The pellet was palpable in his cheek – it could be rolled between the fingers. To remove it was surely a simple thing, and one which I, Webby, the future doctor, was best placed to carry out. We acquired a razor blade, and a flannel to mop the blood, and an appointed time was fixed when staff were least likely to be around. The patient was on the bed, with a boy at each corner to restrain him, and one at the dormitory door on look-out duty, and the razor blade was poised to strike, when he suddenly acquired an affection for his pellet. He would prefer it to remain in his cheek, he insisted. My surgical skills had, sadly, to await another day.

A day that we all dreaded, whether we admitted it or not, was the day of our annual TAB (typhoid) injections. The news was kept from us until the last moment, to avoid rising panic. We were done a dormitory at a time, queuing nervously while the san matron, in her starched white uniform and frilly cap, wielded her long, blunt, stainless steel needles. The smell of antiseptic pervaded the air. We queued in alphabetical order, so I was always near the end, and had the agony of watching those ahead submit to the executioner. 'Does it hurt? Does it hurt?' we anxiously asked each victim, knowing full well that it did. Every now and then our anxiety reached a crescendo when a boy – usually a particularly tough and gung-ho boy – would faint, or be laid down in a sweaty pallor. That night, at bath time, we would compare arms. Whose was the reddest? Who had had the worst reaction? Who blubbed? And we would hope that our sore arms were better before the next games time. The bullies of the school took the opportunity to punch us on our upper arms, right where they were sorest.

Although I had made up my mind to become a doctor, I had no love whatever for the sanatorium. It was the place where unpleasant things happened; the place that combined the smell of antiseptics and floor polish; the place of sharp needles and shiny threatening instruments and starched white sheets. So when I began to feel really ill one day I said nothing, and hoped it would go away. But it didn't go away. I felt sick. Food tasted strange. I shivered uncontrollably. And then I began to turn

The Webster family in front of our home.

an odd colour. I could hide it no longer. I was ordered to the san, and diagnosed with infectious hepatitis. A period of isolation followed in the san. I was a prisoner, gazing out at my friends playing on the distant, sunny sports fields. But the day finally came when I was once again a normal colour, and I was released. Every cloud has a silver lining. The school doctor said that I must eat no fat at all for several months. Ma Simpy came to the rescue, with a wonderful, carbohydrate-rich diet. Instead of butter I had lashings of jam and honey, and many other treats. I was almost sorry to get well.

Living as we did in Marsabit we were well out of range of any dentist, and did not have the regular checks that we should have had. On one occasion when a painful tooth flared up in the holidays Dad brought his limited dental skills to bear, and extracted it. The anaesthetic seemed to miss the right spot, and ran down my throat instead. The extraction was not an experience that I wished ever to repeat, and I think that Dad was right, on the whole, to confine himself to ecclesiastical, rather than dental, skills. Following that experience an arrangement was made for me to be taken to a dentist during term time. He was appalled at the state of my teeth, and said that three must be extracted forthwith under general anaesthetic. This involved a wire face mask, a wad of cotton wool and chloroform. I was not minded to co-operate, and leapt off the couch and fled. I was chased round and round a table in the waiting room, to the consternation of waiting patients. I was finally rounded up by the flustered dentist, his nurse, and two receptionists, and was held down while the chloroform took effect. I remember vividly the sensation of falling down a tiled well, from the bottom of which rose a sickly sweet stench – the smell of the chloroform. The terrifying experience confirmed to me that the best way to cope with the whole medical scenario, with all its unpleasant and frightening procedures, was to get involved with it. If you can't beat it, join it.

Nairobi, at an altitude of just under six thousand feet, has really a very healthy climate. But I grew up in an era when it was feared that the rays of the sun were damaging, not to the skin, but to the brain. The climate was thought to be enervating, deleterious to the health. A strict school rule was that at all times when out of doors we had to wear regulation felt hats, to absorb the sun's rays before they could damage our delicate brains. Another strict rule was that of rest time. For one hour after lunch each day, before we went to afternoon lessons, we had to lie on our beds in total silence. We could read or we could sleep. It was at rest times that I discovered the joy of reading – initially Enid Blyton, then the Biggles books, and later I became an avid reader of Charles Dickens. Before each term I would scour the shelves at home for books to take to school. *Robinson Crusoe, Grimm's Fairy Tales, Gulliver's Travels* – so many of the classics – came with me to school. But a big mistake was *Little Women*. That made me the laughing stock of the dormitory. I pushed it to the back of my locker, and it never did get read.

After compulsory letter writing on Saturdays we were free to play and roam in the extensive school compound. We soon formed gangs, as boys do. We played cowboys and Indians, made dens, scrumped loquats from a garden next door, and played endless games of dinkies, marbles and hopscotch. I became intrigued by ants. I would lie for hours on my stomach, watching them scurry to and from their holes, carrying grass seed, or crumbs that I fed them. Sometimes I fed them a grasshopper, and watched as they dismembered it, reducing the parts to a size that would fit down their holes. If the bits did not fit they would put them aside while they enlarged their hole, pushing up 'boulders' several times their own size. I was intrigued by the way they communicated with one another. If an ant happened on a large morsel of food it would spend time sizing it up, and then rush homewards, touching feelers with any colleague it met. Within minutes there would be a whole bevy of ants bustling round the food, and cooperating to shift it. I, aged seven, recorded my observations in true Darwinian style, and in due course banged out, on Dad's old typewriter, a small booklet called, appropriately, *Ants*. It was never published, but I still have it.

Baboon, or trap-door, spiders were other inhabitants of our playing fields. We called them, wrongly, tarantulas. These large, hairy spiders lived in holes in the ground, and could be taunted and teased to the surface with grass stalks. They had fearsome pincers, and a poisonous bite. They appealed to our baser boyish instincts. We would tickle their holes, tempt them to the surface, and then trap them in a tin. 'Tarantula' fights then took place, as those 'owned' by different boys were set on one another. It was always a fight to the death, and the victorious spider would be smuggled in to the dormitory, and kept in a tin in the owner's bedside locker until the next tournament. From time to time Ma E, when checking our lockers for tidiness and contraband, would have a terrible fright on checking a sweet tin. We felt that the fright was a just reward for prying.

Dennis, David and Marilyn having fun in the tin bath.

Ants and baboon spiders often had us lying on our stomachs in the hot sun, hats pulled down over our heads, prodding and poking. So too did antlions, the larvae of dragon flies. These little grey creatures, with small heads and huge pincers, burrow backwards in to the sandy soil, creating a conical crater, at the bottom of which they lurk, hidden except for their pincers. Unsuspecting ants happen along, slip into the crater, are prevented from climbing out by the antlion flicking soil with its head, and as they fall to the bottom of the crater the victims are grasped by the pincers, dragged under the soil and devoured. Antlions are, again, a boy's, rather than a girl's, insect – providing all the thrills of a deadly spectator sport. We often kept tins of antlions in our lockers, alongside the baboon spiders, and brought ants in to the dormitory to feed them.

It was not only the quality of soap that distinguished a mishkid. My toothpaste was of a basic variety, and my clothes almost invariably Dennis's cast-offs. On the only occasion when I had a brand new school blazer it was stolen from the car, outside the clothing store, within minutes of buying it. It was a case of back to second hand. So it was embarrassing, though not altogether surprising, when a boy whose affluent parents lived in Zanzibar said to me one day, 'Webby, next term I'm going to bring you some clothes.'

'No, I'm okay!' I protested, thinking how impoverished I must look.

'I'd like to,' he insisted. 'Definitely, next term!' Next term arrived, and he said, 'I've brought you those clothes.'

I felt awkward, the object of charity. He handed me a package – a very small package. A tie? A handkerchief? I opened it not knowing what I was going to find. And there was an envelope – of cloves! Zanzibar's prime export. He must have wondered why I had protested about a few cloves.

That was not the only word I got wrong. My mishkid friend George and I came by some shocking but priceless information. Somehow we discovered the correct anatomical word for the male appendage. In normal school parlance it went by a number of names, of which the politest was *willy*. But we discovered the proper name. This was astounding stuff, especially for two mishkids to have such exclusive knowledge. We decided that the most effective way to amaze and shock our friends, and to demonstrate our worldliness, would be to call the word out loud in the playground. So it was that one day, in the middle of a game of dinkies, we both called out loudly 'Pencil!' The reaction from other boys around us was stunningly indifferent. There was not even a glance. Not a twitch. We tried again, with an equally disappointing result. Perhaps the world was not yet ready for our superior knowledge. Fortunately our error became apparent long before I entered medical school, where it really would have been embarrassing.

CHAPTER NINE

Adventure was built in to our lives. Every journey to and from Marsabit was an excitement. Our home was probably more remote than that of any of our school mates, and we were proud of it. But sometimes the journey became just too much of an adventure. Such as our journey home from school in 1949. We always carried two spare wheels, but on that occasion repeated punctures meant that Dad had to set to at the roadside to repair them. Removing the wheel was simple enough, but breaking the seal of the tyre was a challenge – especially the large, heavy duty tyres. In Isiolo we bought a new puncture repair outfit. Seventy miles on and we had yet another puncture – or perhaps it was the previous patch coming off. When Dad came to open the new puncture repair outfit he discovered that the rubber solution was solid – it had perished in the hot *duka* in Isiolo. We were in trouble. The sun was blazing down and there was not a scrap of shade. In desperation we tore up thorn bushes, and crammed them into the tyre, but on releasing the jack they crumbled to dust. There were two priorities – shade and water. The dry Merille river bed lay just two miles ahead. There we would have the shade of doum palms, and possibly water if we dug in the sandy river bed. We drove on slowly on the flat tyre. But soon the rough stony road was slicing up the tyre, and grinding on the wheel rim. We came to a halt one mile short of the river bed, but alongside a long rocky outcrop, and one shady acacia tree. Here we decided to stay, until another vehicle might happen along.

Dad recalled that someone had once told him that occasionally water could be found in these rocks. It seemed unlikely, but Dennis and I set off, with all the adventurous spirit of a Livingstone or a Stanley. And there, in a hollow in the rocks, we found a pool of water. Greenish water, but who were we to fuss? It was water! It was five days before another vehicle came along – five days of relentless sun, beating down on, and reflected off, those rocks. That water, and the thin shade of our acacia tree, were life-saving. By day we would climb to the top of the rocks to look out over the thornbush plains for tell-tale signs of dust – which would signal an approaching vehicle. At night, before settling down to sleep in our camp beds next to the fire, we would make one last check, for the lights of an approaching vehicle. There was nothing but a dome of stars above and inky darkness around, pierced by the howl of a hyena, or the crack of a bush as something moved in the undergrowth. A rhino visited our camp one night, and frightened us with a loud snort. An elephant browsed on a tree not far from us one day. Hyraxes cavorted in and out of the nooks and crannies in the rocks. Weaver birds twittered in their nests in the acacia branches above us. But there was no sign of human life.

Then on the fifth day we saw a column of dust to the north. 'A rescue! A rescue!' Dennis and I shouted excitedly. It was a lorry from Marsabit. Mum had asked the driver to look out for us. She knew that we had passed Isiolo – a telegram from Isiolo had confirmed that we had signed the book at the barrier. She guessed that it might be tyre trouble, and had given the lorry driver a collection of every tyre in our store at Marsabit. But all were the wrong size. Mum had also sent us a basket of fruit from the garden, in case our supplies were short. The driver of the lorry took a message from us to a friendly Pathan trader in Isiolo, Mr Khan, explaining our problem. Though ill with malaria he immediately got up from his sick bed and set out with a spare wheel and new puncture repair outfit, and arrived late that evening. At last we could continue our journey north. On the edge of the Kaisut desert we had yet another puncture. We could now repair that – but the tyre pump broke! We had to wait for Mr Khan, who was following some distance behind, to catch up with us. In the meantime Dad, exhausted, slept. While he slept in his seat a hyena snuffled around the wheels of the car, but fortunately did not chew them. We finally arrived home in the early hours of Easter Sunday. A pressure lamp was burning in the window – a welcome home from Mum who knew that wherever we were, whatever had happened, sooner or later we would come. We stoked up the Dover stove, brewed tea, and recounted our adventure around the pressure lamp. It was good to be home. It was a life of uncertainty, but uncertainty made bearable by faith.

1952 was the year of the floods. The long rainy season began in March, and it continued to rain – day after day it rained, always in the afternoon. The sky over Nairobi would turn black, the air still and heavy as though nature was holding its breath. Then suddenly an ominous rumble, which echoed and re-echoed around the hill on which the school stood. And then the rain – at first fat drops hitting the ground, and soon a drumming deluge. Roads turned to rivers. Ditches became torrents of red soil-stained water, like networks of arteries. Playing fields turned to lakes. Nobody remembered rain and floods like it, and they were widespread over Kenya. And we had a problem. Dad had come down from Marsabit for meetings before the rains began. Now it was time to take us back to Marsabit for the Easter holidays. But reports were not good. The rivers in the NFD were in full spate. Bridges had been washed away. In places the road had been cut in two by deep gulleys. The Kaisut desert was one vast lake. There was no way that any vehicle could reach Marsabit by road. We drove as far as Nanyuki, hoping that the rivers and floods might have subsided, but the rain continued relentlessly. We began to wonder if we would ever get home that holiday, or see Mum. But Dad had a plan. He contacted a pilot, Mr Turner-Dauncey, who agreed to fly us to Marsabit in his four-seater plane, and at the same time to take post and some necessary supplies. Such flights were unusual in those days, and for us it was definitely a first. Another adventure! So we took off from Nanyuki's grass air strip, and were soon flying over bushland turned vivid green by rain. Red-brown rivers snaked through the bush. We swooped low over herds of buck and giraffe and elephant, revelling in the lushness. And as we came in to Marsabit he took us low over our house at Karantina, and we saw Mum waving frantically. We were home again! By the end of that holiday the road was still impassable. Mr Turner-Dauncey flew us to Nairobi, where he banked low over his own house, standing like an island in a lake. 1952 was indeed the year of the floods.

Dennis and David with Mr Turner-Dauncey's plane at the Marsabit airstrip.

Rain delayed our return to school on at least one other occasion. Parts of the Kaisut desert were under water, and for long stretches we walked in the deep ruts of the Dodge, to lighten the load. As we approached the Milgis, usually a dry stony river bed in the Kaisut, we heard a roaring noise, as of heavy traffic on a highway. It was the Milgis in flood. And gathered on the north bank milled thousands of sheep and goats, stranded on their way down country to market. We could no more cross the Milgis than they could. We set up our camp beds at the side of the car, and fell asleep to the sound of the roar of the river mingled with the bleating of the animals. By morning the level of the river had fallen enough for us to cross. As school was our destination Dennis and I were not at all sure that we were glad to get across. But thirty miles on we were delighted to find the Merrille river also in full flood, and the approaches to the bridge washed away. Now there was no option but to turn round and make our way back to

Wading through the flooded Milgis in the Kaisut Desert.

Marsabit. Our school holiday had been extended. It was several more days before news came that the Merrille was now passable, though we had to drive through the river bed, the bridge being unusable. We laid branches of doum palms in the river banks, and waded in to the river to check its depth. Our cheers, as the Dodge surged through the water and soft sand in four wheel drive, were somewhat muted – there was nothing now to prevent us from getting to school.

The Kaisut desert, normally a burning, barren wasteland, with lava rock outcrops hurled in the past from the volcanic craters of Marsabit, is transformed beyond recognition by rain. Where normally dust devils snake across the bare desert floor, sucking bits of dry thornscrub into the hot air like giant vacuum cleaners, and where mirages shimmer on the desert surface, after rain a flower garden appears. The desert is carpeted with flowers whose seeds have lain dormant in the sand. Daisies in their millions nod their heads in the breeze, lilies burst from the desert crust, and wild convolvulus twines its way over acacia shrubs. As Isaiah says:

> The desert and the parched land will be glad;
> the wilderness will rejoice and blossom.
> Like the crocus, it will burst into bloom …
>
> *Isaiah 35:1–2 (NIV)*

Memories of those journeys to and from Marsabit crowd in. On occasion we drove into thick clouds of locusts, migrating from their breeding grounds in the horn of Africa. The sky would darken, and the windscreen wipers work at full speed to clear the orange-red fluid from the car's screen, as thousands of locusts splattered against it. Sometimes we came across vast swarms of locust hoppers – the immature forms that have not yet grown wings. As fast as the car's wheels squashed them thousands more crawled over the bodies and filled the gap. These were locusts heading south, to feed off and decimate the *shambas* of farmers in the more fertile regions. Over the years the Department of Locust Control did an effective job in reducing this menace.

It was creatures somewhat larger than locusts that we encountered more often on those journeys. There was the time when we stopped to pitch camp after dark, and had no sooner put up our camp beds than we heard the cracking of branches all around us, and deep rumbling sounds. We had pitched camp in the middle of a herd of elephants. It took considerably less time to dismantle camp than it had taken to set it up. We usually chose our camp site very carefully – a place with dead wood for the fire, a clearing in the bush, and a breeze to minimise mosquitoes. On one school trip we were given a lift by the head of the Public Works Department, a Mr Porter and his wife. They chose a rather low-lying camp site, and the mosquitoes were terrible. By morning I was so badly bitten that, in Mrs Porter's words, you could not have put a pin between the bites on my face. That was not a good state in which to return to school – and the consequence, some days later, was a bout of malaria, and another spell in the san.

The only local driver that our parents were happy to entrust us to was Mr Khan, the one who rescued us at Merrille. He was famed for the carefulness and slowness of his driving – intended primarily to conserve his lorry on those destructive roads. His nick-name was 'Bwana Pole-pole', Mr Slow. We felt safe perched on the goods on the back of Mr Khan's lorry, but the journey seemed to take for ever as he eased his lorry over potholes and through river beds, and we swayed and lurched from side to side. On one occasion Mr Khan handed us on at Isiolo to a sheep lorry. The back of the lorry, where our school trunks were put, was crammed with sheep heading for market. We sat up front, in the cab. By the time we arrived at railhead, at Nanyuki, our trunks were coated with a thick, acrid layer of sheep droppings. There was no opportunity to clean them before they went in to the luggage van of the train, and they arrived in the dormitory at school still crusted and very pungent. We were not popular with our dormitory mates, but then what else could one expect of mishkids? Cheap soap, second hand clothes, and trunks that smelt like a farmyard.

CHAPTER TEN

Even in a thorn tree beautiful birds nest. And similarly at Nairobi Primary School, though generally I found the regime harsh and thorny, there were beautiful exceptions – touches of kindness, times of happiness. Ma Simpy, in the dining room, was a case in point. So too was Ma Parky. She was our Cub Leader – or, in the correct jargon, Akela. Every week, eyes shining with enthusiasm through her thick glasses, and her woggle askew, she would exhort us to: 'DYB, DYB, DYB' ('Do Your Best').

And it was to her that we chanted back that we would: 'DOB, DOB, DOB' ('Do Our Best').

When George and I found a tortoise wandering across the playing fields we adopted it, and took it back to the dormitory. But a bedside locker is not the best place to keep a tortoise. It needed walks. It needed green stuff to eat. It left smelly deposits. And it was not long before our dormitory matron discovered our new friend, and furiously ordered it out, and us with it. We had a problem. But Ma Parky lived in a flat on the school compound, and we decided to introduce her to our tortoise, and see if by any chance she would 'Do Her Best' for us. She was wonderful. She offered him (or was it her?) a home, and an invitation for us to visit every Saturday. George and I would take our tortoise out for a walk – a very slow walk – and return to a treat of squash and biscuits. It is debatable whether the main attraction each Saturday was our tortoise or the refreshments – or even Ma Parky herself.

Ma W was my French teacher. She was plump, and kindly and homely. Our relationship was good until the day I spoiled it. I drew in the back of my French vocabulary book a picture of Ma W – a picture of which I was quite proud, and which I felt to be quite a good likeness, quite flattering in fact, demonstrating well her ample proportions. Perhaps foolishly I actually labelled the picture 'Ma W' – not a wise move in a book that she regularly took in for marking. Inevitably she came across my artwork, and was not amused. I was ordered to take the book forthwith to our formidable headmaster, the Reverend 'Moony' B, and to show him what I had done. The Reverend Moony was noted for his ready use of the cane. I did not particularly want to experience his cane. I had to think fast. Our classrooms were temporary wooden buildings, raised on piles. There was space to crawl underneath. I took full advantage of this space, and slithered under the classroom. I lay there for a while – the sort of time it would have taken to get to Moony's office and receive a caning – then I crawled out, dusted myself down, and returned to the classroom with an appropriately remorseful look.

'So, what did he say?' asked Ma W.

'He told me never, ever, to do such a thing again!' I lied.

She gave me a long, somewhat doubtful look, but thankfully must have decided that a mishkid would surely tell the truth. If only she knew!

Another teacher who brought kindness into my life was Pa Turner. The Reverend (yes, another reverend) Turner followed the bully Bucksarse as our housemaster. He also taught history and Latin. Unlike Bucksarse, who seemed to hate mishkids, Pa Turner went out of his way to be kind. He lent me books, and on one occasion (following a satisfactory Latin test) he said I could choose and keep any book I wished from his bookcase. I had just finished reading his gripping story of the plague and fire of London, and longed to take that. But for some extraordinary and pious reason I chose a Revised Version of the Bible – a book I still have, but a version that I have never used. It was a wasted opportunity.

Pa Turner had a fascinating habit. When dictating notes to us he would occupy the pauses, while we were writing, by slowly protruding his bottom pair of dentures with his tongue. The gleaming set would emerge from above his lower lip, further and further, while our concentration was torn between them and our notes. When they were on the verge of falling out there would be a sudden sharp suck, and with a clack the dentures would fly back into place in readiness for the next sentence. We lived for the day when the dentures would fall out, but unfortunately Pa Turner had mastered the skill of brinkmanship.

Although our boarding houses were segregated between the sexes, our classes were mixed. My class was graced with the presence of two mishkid girls, the Bostock twins, both blonde, and the daughters of an Archdeacon no less. I could never make out which twin was Joy and which was Jane, but one of them sat in the desk in front of me. Her long, blonde plaits fell temptingly before my eyes. I discovered that if I lifted a plait very gently I could place the tip of it in my inkwell, and then return it to its rightful place, without its owner knowing. The blue Quink ink showed up well on the lovely blonde hair.

Another girl in my year, Ann, became the heart-throb of us boys. Of course in our early years at primary school we boys had no time at all for girls. They played sissy games, and we and they kept to ourselves. We roared our dinkies through the dust; they skipped to the rhythm of dainty songs. We shot one another dead in games of Cowboys and Indians; they gathered in sedate groups in the shade of a tree, to dress and tend their dolls. But by our last year, at the age of eleven, girls suddenly became more interesting. Or perhaps we became more interested. Or both. And Ann was more interesting than most. She had a natural aptitude for flirting, and knew how to keep boys at tantalising arm's length. I imagined that it would be a handsome, tanned, muscular son of a settler who would finally win her heart. So it came as a shock to learn that my mishkid friend George – podgy, freckly George – had become the official boyfriend of Ann. I must admit to twinges – no, pangs – of jealousy. Then events took an unexpected turn. I found in my desk one day a small package. I opened it, and there lay one of my handkerchiefs, washed, ironed and neatly folded, and emitting a faint but pleasant scent. I had no idea who had come by it, or how. But then, a day or two later, came a short but sweet love letter from 'Jacqueline'. The mystery was solved. Jacqueline was Ann's best friend. George was my best friend. And as George and Ann were now an 'item', Jacqueline obviously saw a future for herself and me. She was a nice enough girl – tall, very freckly, with long plaits. But I would have preferred the excitement of Ann. The four of us used to have trysts behind the classrooms on Saturday afternoons. We talked a little, but, apart from Ann, we were very shy. I don't think we ever even touched hands. We certainly never kissed. And the lack of mutual interests soon brought our tentative romances to a premature end.

Christianity played a large part in the life of the school – though it was a Government, not a church, school. Sunday mornings saw the whole school wending its way, in crocodile fashion, down the hill to All Saints Cathedral. Only Roman Catholics, Jews, and Afrikaner children (who belonged to the Dutch Reformed Church) were exempt. The rest of us sat through a fairly traditional Anglican service. I actually liked the cathedral. I liked its dark, cool, cavernous interior. I liked the grey stones. I knew that I had been baptised there. The Provost, the Very Reverend Evan Hopkins, was a friend of Dad. And when an appeal was made to pay for an extension to the cathedral, I donated the price of one stone, five whole shillings, one quarter of my term's pocket money, for the cause. When the extension was complete I used to sit and gaze at the stones, and wonder which one was mine. I am still not sure.

Sunday afternoons were taken up with Crusaders, a non-denominational Christian movement for children. This was voluntary, but I knew that my parents would wish me to go. That too was enjoyable

The outside of the All Saints Cathedral, Nairobi.

Inside All Saints Cathedral, Nairobi.

– a good sing, a talk and games. The small boys' class was run by a little Scotsman, Mr Craig, who called us his *jewels*. I wasn't sure that I wanted to be a jewel, and certainly did not share that information with my non-Crusader friends. Classes for bigger boys were led by Hugh Sansom, and Sue, who became his wife. The names Hugh and Sue went well together, and in due course we named our budgies after them.

On Sunday evenings we became Anglicans again, with Evensong in the school hall. Each weekday morning school began with a religious assembly in the open sided, pillared hall, beneath the clock tower. RE lessons were called Scripture lessons, and we learned Bible stories, and Christian basics. On top of all this our parents signed us up for Sunday School by post. A booklet of Bible stories and questions would arrive each month, and I would spend some rest times filling in the answers to post back. The answers were so obvious that each month I scored full marks, and a 'prize' – usually something like a card with a Bible text. I would have preferred something edible. With all this imposed Christianity it is perhaps surprising that I did not rebel. I think to a large extent I submitted to it out of loyalty to Mum and Dad. I knew that it would please them. But at this stage in my life it did not really mean very much to me. It was a routine, as comfortable as an old slipper, but with little impact on my life. But it was laying foundations for which I would later be grateful.

Perhaps the most anxiety-provoking school service was the one when the headmaster invited Dad to preach. On the one hand I was proud that it would be my father speaking to the school. But on the other I was terrified that he would be boring, or would be laughed at. Dad had various mannerisms and tics, dating back to chorea in his childhood. I dreaded them becoming obvious to my schoolmates. I knew that I would never hear the end of it. So it was with an agonising mixture of pride and dread that I watched him process in to the hall, in his clerical robes, led by the headmaster. But I need not have feared. I can remember to this day what he preached about. It was about faith. It was the story of Blondin, and how he pushed someone in a wheelbarrow across a tightrope over the Niagara Falls. That passenger had no option but to have faith in Blondin, and to sit back and put his life in Blondin's hands. So with God. At the end of the service several boys said, 'Your Pa was good, Webby!' That was praise indeed, and I relaxed into a warm glow of pride. Dad had passed the test.

A highlight of 1952 was the royal visit to Kenya of Princess Elizabeth and her spouse the Duke of Edinburgh. For their wedding, in 1947, the people of Kenya had given them a hunting lodge, on the Sagana river in the Aberdare mountains. Until now they had not had the opportunity to visit it. Now they had come. Nairobi was bedecked with flags and bunting. Instant flowerbeds appeared on every roundabout in the city. There was a great atmosphere of expectation and festivity. The Princess and Duke said goodbye to King George VI at London airport on 31st January, knowing him to be recovering from a lung cancer operation. They flew in to Nairobi, and stayed with the Governor, Sir Philip Mitchell, at Government House – an imposing building just across the road from our school. On Sunday 4th February they were due to drive up to Sagana Lodge. The ninety miles of earth road to Sagana had been sprayed with water to lay the dust. The flags and bunting from Nairobi had been rushed upcountry, to greet the royal couple there. Mum had come down from Marsabit for the occasion, and we stood with her at the gates of Government House. Princess Elizabeth graced us with a smile and a wave as they set off on their journey.

Two days later I was in a Latin lesson with the headmaster when a grave-faced boy interrupted the lesson with a message for him. We overheard the words: 'Please Sir! The King is dead!' The King had died in his sleep from an embolus. The Princess meanwhile was viewing game from Treetops Hotel near Sagana. It fell to the Duke of Edinburgh to break the news to her at Sagana the next day. Her visit to Kenya was cut short, and she and the Duke flew straight back to England. That young, happy Princess who had waved to us just two days previously was now Queen of Great Britain and all her Dominions. The following year both Mum and Dad were awarded, by His Excellency the Governor, Sir Evelyn Baring, the Coronation Medal, in recognition of their work for the colony. Mum – never one for any kind of pomp and ceremony – put her medal away in a drawer. But at the next official occasion in Marsabit the District Commissioner asked her why she was not wearing her medal. He said that in future she must. So she did – but always took care to wear a coat over it! Neither Mum nor Dad ever sought recognition or praise for what they did.

It was the evening of 21st October, 1952, when a message came round to the dormitories at bath time – the whole boarding house was to congregate in the common room for a special announcement. Excitement ran high. What could it be? What spectacular misdemeanour had someone committed? The headmaster himself, the Reverend 'Moony', was there. It must be something very serious. He told us, in solemn tones, that a State of Emergency throughout the Colony had been declared that very day by the newly appointed Governor of Kenya, Sir Evelyn Baring. He told us how a seditious and violent secret Kikuyu society, called Mau Mau, was at work. Its aim was to oust all whites from Kenya, and to recover the 'stolen' white highlands. Sixty Kikuyu loyal to the Government, including the Kikuyu chief, Waruhiu, had been murdered. He told us that 'an evil and dangerous man, Jomo Kenyatta, was the ringleader, and that he and his henchmen had been arrested that day under the new emergency regulations. British troops of the Black Watch were on their way to reinforce the Kenya Regiment, King's African Rifles and Kenya Police. He implied that all this action was long overdue, and that it had needed the new Governor to take a firm hand. New school rules were announced. We were on no account allowed out of the boarding house after dark. We must at all times move around the school compound in groups of no less than five. There were new restrictive rules about leave-outs and shopping trips. It was all a bit scary, and yet gave us a frisson of excitement. We wondered what lay ahead.

CHAPTER ELEVEN

Holidays, in the sense of going away somewhere other than home, were something we did not experience until my last year at Nairobi Primary School, 1952. We did not resent it. There was nowhere in the world we would rather spend our holidays than at Marsabit. Other boys talked about exciting trips to game parks. We lived in a game park. We had elephant and buffalo and greater kudu on our doorstep. We did not need to go to game parks. But I did feel envious when my friends talked about holidays at the coast. I had very vague memories of Malindi when I was small. But my only real memories of seaside were of Blackpool in 1947. The Kenya coast sounded a whole lot better than Blackpool. Boys spoke of glistening white sands, and coral reefs and rustling palms. They talked of big game fishing, and snorkelling on the reef. Yes, I was envious. But with our parents on a missionary 'allowance' (it was not given the dignity of the word 'salary') of about £200 a year coast holidays were out of the question. It was just part of the reality of being a mishkid.

Then in 1952 surprise followed surprise. Farmers at Timau, near Nanyuki, needed some holiday themselves, and wanted someone reliable to 'farm-sit' for them. No experience of farming was necessary. And so we found ourselves enjoying two free weeks on an extensive farm, Arden Capel, on the slopes of Mount Kenya. The African farm manager saw to all the day-to-day running of the farm – the dipping of the sheep, milking of cows, slopping out of pigs, grooming of horses. We just enjoyed watching, and even joining in, farm activities. Dennis and I had hundreds of acres on which to roam, crystal clear icy streams to dam, horses we could ride

Dennis, Marilyn and David in the stream at the Timau farm.

Dennis and David riding the farm horses.

bare foot. We feasted on fresh farm cream and butter and meat. It was bliss. The only slight tension was the rather cool attitude towards us of the manager. We assumed that he resented having agriculturally ignorant white people supposedly in charge of his farm. It was understandable. It was not until several months later, after the state of emergency had been declared, that we discovered that the manager had, all along, been a Mau Mau oath administrator, conducting horrific oathing ceremonies under our very noses. One of the very first overt atrocities carried out by Mau Mau was later that year on the neighbouring farm to Arden Capel. A herd of pedigree cattle belonging to the white farmer was hamstrung, and left to die an agonising death.

We had a second free holiday that same year. Arthur and Sophie Whibley offered us a free fortnight at their guest house on the creek on Mombasa island. Arthur, known affectionately by many missionaries as 'Uncle Arthur', or 'Klarfur' for short, had given Mum away at her wedding in Nairobi in 1937. She had only met him two days previously. But her own father could not be there, and Klarfur stood in. He was white-haired, jolly and fatherly. So in the August of 1952 we had the excitement of an overnight train journey from Nairobi to the coast. It was sheer joy to be sleeping on a train that was not heading for school. We woke at

Uncle Arthur and Auntie Sophie.

intervals through the night as the train squealed and groaned to a stop at little one-eyed stations, with names that seemed to fit the rhythm of the wheels on the rails. Kiboko, Makindu, Kibwezi, Tsavo and Voi. We peered out to see platform hawkers selling tea from steaming urns, and piles of fresh-fried *mandasi* cakes. As the new day dawned we let down the mosquito netting shutters and leaned out of the windows, braving the smuts from the steam engine, to see who would be the first to spy a coconut palm. Soon we were passing groves of coconut palms and cashew nut trees. The smell of the sea mingled with the smoke of the train. Over the causeway and on to Mombasa island we steamed, and there was Klarfur to meet us, his white hair escaping from under his jaunty Panama hat.

In the creek at Mombasa.

The Whibley's guest house stood on a cliff overlooking the creek which surrounds the island of Mombasa. Across the creek, in a grove of coconut palms, lay Freretown, the site where the early CMS missionaries had first settled, and built a refuge for freed slaves. Down the creek, towards the open sea, lay the Old Harbour, busy with dhows from Arabia and Zanzibar, the bearers of cloth and rugs and spices and other exotic goods. Our room, at the base of the house, opened through French windows onto a steep path which zig-zagged down to the beach past straggling bougainvilleas, riotous with purple and red and orange. Frangipani bushes filled the air with scent. We were in heaven. The sandy beach was secluded but small, hemmed in at either end with mangroves. It shelved steeply in to the warm and deep water of the creek. It was on that holiday that I taught myself to swim.

Also staying was another missionary family, from Uganda, with three sons, the younger two about our ages. The oldest son, John, was already a senior at the secondary school in Nairobi, the Prince of Wales, to which Dennis had already moved, and for which I was destined the following year. It emerged that he would be the head boy of my house, Grigg. It seemed a happy coincidence that, not only did Dennis and I have companions of our own age for the holiday, but that my head of house would be someone I had already met and had befriended. All five of us organised a sports day on the beach, and had a wonderful holiday together. But I was to be severely disillusioned by John the next year.

Our stay in Mombasa coincided with the Kenya Coast Schools Music Festival at Tononoka. Schools from up and down the coast had entered choirs. Each choir had to sing two songs – an indigenous song of their choice, and the set piece, which was, bizarrely, the traditional

English melody 'Early one morning, just as the sun was rising.' Choir after choir sang with great expression and gusto, 'O! Don't deceive me! O! Never leave me! How could you use a poor maiden so?' How many understood about 'bowers' and 'vows to be true' I am not sure. But any lack of understanding was more than made up for by passion. It was their own tribal songs though that really came from the heart. Sung in close harmony, with the backdrop of blue sky and waving palms, the sound was hauntingly beautiful, and still echoes in my memory.

1952 should have been a good year. Two free holidays! At school I was now a senior, and a prefect, all of ten, going on eleven, years old. I was doing well in class, and was expected to pass the Kenya Preliminary Examinations (KPE) for entry to secondary school with flying colours. But a cloud loomed over my life. Something that troubled me deeply, but which I did not feel able to tell anyone about. Pa Turner, our housemaster, had gone on leave to England. We had an acting housemaster, Mr H. He was young and tall and handsome, with curly hair. He was engaged to be married, and we studied with interest his glamorous fiancée, when she came to visit him. He was a popular teacher, and taught me geography and maths. Then one evening, on his nightly round of the dormitories before lights-out, he came across a boy in my dormitory who had accidentally pulled out the cord of his pyjamas, and was trying to thread it through again. Mr H offered to do it for him, but did it in such a way that he paid an unusual amount of attention to that area of the boy's anatomy. It seemed very odd. I began to notice that Mr H came stealthily around the dormitories again after lights-out, long after most boys were asleep. Then one night I was woken by a torch shining in my face. I sat up with a start. It was Mr H. 'Would you like to come to my flat and see your excellent marks for your last prep?' he whispered. Odder and odder. I obediently donned my dressing gown, and followed him along the dark and silent verandah to his flat, wondering why the marks for my prep had assumed such urgency. And so the sexual abuse began. Always he offered glacier mints. The smell of them brings back the memory. I was confused. I was ashamed and embarrassed. I felt guilty. I was afraid. Mr H held a lot of power over my life and my future – he would write my final report; he could perhaps influence the outcome of the KPE exams (or so I feared). And he was a good teacher. He was popular with the boys. I knew it was wrong, yet if it was wrong why did a teacher whom I trusted and respected do it? What would happen to me if I spoke against him? Would my friends send me to Coventry? And even more confusing, much as I hated and dreaded those nights, yet in a strange way there was a sense of being flattered; of being chosen. I was in a turmoil, and I did not know who to tell, or how to tell. Pa Turner was not there. Moony, the headmaster, was scary, and I felt, in some distorted way, that he might blame me. I knew for sure my parents would be very upset, and I didn't want to cause them hurt. When, in cases of sexual abuse, others say 'Why on earth didn't you say something?' they don't understand the subtle pressures at play. So I said nothing to anyone. It became my dreadful secret, and each night I hoped and prayed that that torch would not shine in my face.

I passed the KPE. My friend and rival, Tim, beat me to first place in the school. I came ninth in the Colony. And so in January 1953 I began a new life at the Prince of Wales School. There were new friends to be made from other primary schools. It was altogether a tougher world. Our prefects seemed huge, and they shaved, and had deep voices, and were allowed to smoke in their common room. From being seniors and prefects in our junior schools we were now suddenly again the lowest

The Prince of Wales School, Nairobi.

of the low, 'rabble'. We had to make the prefects' beds and clean their shoes. Ours was never to reason why, ours was but to do and, sometimes we felt like it, die. We began our time in secondary school in Junior House – a collection of pre-war Nissen huts. In the second year we would move to another collection of wooden huts, Intermediate House. Then for our final four years we would move on to our respective senior houses, of which there were six. I was in Grigg House, named after a former Governor of Kenya.

1953 was the year when Mum and Dad were once again due for home leave in England. They would be gone for six months. They gave Dennis and me a choice. We could go with them, but then stay on in England at boarding school – in which case we would see them at most once a year thereafter. Or we could stay in Kenya, in which case we would spend our next holidays with our missionary aunt, Edith. Without hesitation we opted for the latter. Dad and Mum came to school to say goodbye. They and three-year-old Marilyn were due to sail from Mombasa in a few days time. It was not an easy goodbye. I was still unsettled in the new school, and we were all experiencing bullying by our prefects. But I was now a big boy, and big boys don't cry – at least not in the sight of other boys.

The very next day I was called out of class, and told to go to the house of the headmaster, Mr P Fletcher, called affectionately 'Jake' or 'Flaky'. I noticed that one or two other boys who had been with me at Nairobi Primary had also been called out at intervals during the morning. What was going on? I was shown into the head's sitting room by Jake himself, and left with a kindly but solemn faced man.

He began, 'Now I'm a police detective, but don't worry. You are not in trouble. Don't be embarrassed. I know all about willies and …' And so it came out. Mr H had been rumbled. And it seemed that a number of boys had been his victims. I was not alone. So for the first time I could talk about it. I could let go of my awful secret. I could offload it onto someone else. And he listened, and gently reassured me that I had done nothing wrong. He took down his notes. Then Jake took over, and gave me a drink before sending me back to the classroom. I felt such a sense of relief.

My one regret was that it remained a secret from my parents, and I would not see them again for over six months. Or so I thought. But as

I returned from games that evening there was the familiar car outside Junior House, and Dad standing by it. Jake had rung them before they left for Mombasa, and they knew the whole story. I did not need to say anything. We clung to one another, and we both wept. And it was so healing. When he left shortly afterwards I felt so much better about the six months ahead. The dark secret was out and dealt with. There was nothing lurking unspoken between us. Later that term Jake informed us one by one that Mr H had been sentenced to four years in prison, and in a strange way I felt sorry for him. He had destroyed his own life. But he could, if we had so allowed, have destroyed ours too. I didn't want him punished, but I did want him changed, so that such a thing would never happen again.

CHAPTER TWELVE

Junior and Intermediate Houses consisted of wooden Nissen huts strung together by corridors. They were very susceptible to fire. In 1953 the Mau Mau emergency was at its height. Threats had been made to kill white schoolchildren, and we were sitting targets for an arson attack. So games periods, during our first term at the Prince of Wales, were spent instead building high protective mud walls around Junior and Intermediate Houses. On the outside of the walls barbed wire fences were erected. Adjacent to each boarding house a watch tower with search lights was set up. Each day at sunset a contingent of armed guards arrived at school, and they manned the watchtowers and patrolled the fences. The same rules applied as at primary school – nobody was to leave the boarding house after dark, and in the daytime we had to move around in groups of no fewer than five, and never to leave the school compound. Cross country races were cancelled when a boy was attacked in a nearby coffee plantation. Our teachers were all armed, and it was quite normal to be taught by a man with a ·45 revolver at his waist. The lady teachers carried more discrete and dainty automatics in their handbags.

All these precautions were necessary, and there were no incidents of boys being attacked at school. One boy in my dormitory was killed in the school holidays, when he stumbled on a group of Mau Mau in the bush near his home. He and a friend were hacked to death with *pangas*. The father of another boy was murdered at the gate of his farm near Nanyuki. But these were the only deaths of white people which directly affected us. We were very aware however of the fighting and violence going on

David and his brother Dennis, taken during David's first year at the Prince of Wales school.

in the country around us. Most of us built crystal sets, to tune in to the local Kenya Broadcasting Corporation, situated right next door to our school. With earphones clamped to our ears we would tickle the crystal with a fine wire until we got reception. Before long transistors became available, and we built transistor sets. The radio reception was much more reliable. We listened daily to the news, usually read by one of our teachers. We heard of murders of white settlers – worrying for those boys whose parents lived on isolated farms. Eric Bowyer (an old man hacked to death in his bath), Bingley, Ferguson, Meikeljohn and Gibson. The list grew. Then there were Mr and Mrs Ruck and their six-year-old son, slaughtered at their farm with *pangas*. The white settlers were under attack. But it was far worse for those Kikuyu who remained loyal to the Government, or who, because of their Christian faith, refused to get involved with the oathing and atrocities of Mau Mau. One of the worst incidents was the Lari massacre when, not many miles from our school, a whole village of one hundred and seventy people, mainly women and children, was torched, and every occupant either hacked or burnt to death. We heard too of operations against the Mau Mau, by a police force and army reinforced by tribal members from northern and western Kenya, and also strongly backed up by British regiments – the Black Watch and the Royal Inniskilling Fusiliers. I kept a record of events in a small red Scout diary. We listened also, after lights out, and with earphones concealed inside our pillowcases, to comedy programmes such as *Beyond Our Ken, Round the Horne* and *Life With the Lyons,* stifling our laughs in our pillows. Funniest of all though were the radio adverts that followed the news. They too were read by some of our teachers, who were obviously paid to sound exuberant about such mundane things as toothpaste and washing powder.

More immediately threatening to us than Mau Mau were our own prefects. There was a culture of bullying, which the headmaster was doing his utmost to change. Prefects still had the authority to cane, but they also indulged in more amusing punishments – such as dragging boys bare-bottomed along the rough coconut matting that ran the length of the dormitories; or making us stand for agonising ages with arms outstretched, balancing heavy books on our palms; or making us write essays on such bizarre subjects as 'The sound a moonbeam makes when it strikes water' – essays which we then had to read out for the entertainment of the prefects in their common room. Worse though than any of our own prefects was my 'friend' John H from the Mombasa holiday, now head of my senior house, Grigg. We juniors, though we all lived together in Junior House, still competed in sports for our respective senior houses. And John H was determined that, in athletics especially, we Grigg juniors, we 'rabble', were going to win. It brought out in him most sadistic instincts. He had us out on the playing fields at sunrise every morning, shouting and screaming at us. We would be compelled to run lap after lap around the field, and then do press-ups and sit-ups until we collapsed. When we collapsed he kicked us back into action. Strong boys were reduced to tears. And John H clearly revelled in his power over us. It was not until these early morning torture sessions came to the attention of our housemaster that they were stopped. It was not altogether surprising that within a few years of leaving school John H was in prison for embezzlement. He was a mishkid sadly gone very wrong.

The Prince of Wales School was one of two Government secondary schools in the colony for white boys – the Duke of York being the other. 'The Princo' as we called ourselves (or 'The Cabbage Patch' as our rivals called us) was, like the Duke of York ('The Duko' or 'The Duck Pond'), a strange hybrid between a public school and a comprehensive. Most white boys, regardless of background or academic ability, went to either the Princo or the Duko. We were streamed throughout the school, and every boy was encouraged to develop his talents, whether academic or practical. We had an outstanding staff, worthy of any public school. A number of them had fought in World War Two and had then, rather than settle back in Blighty, sought perhaps a more adventurous life in the colonies. Heading up the staff was Philip Fletcher, known variously as 'PF', 'Jake' or 'Flakey'. Formerly a senior master at Cheltenham College, he had seen that school through various crises – including three changes of headmaster, and the evacuation of the school to Shrewsbury during the war. A man of deep faith and high principles, he was appointed head of the Prince of Wales after the war. He had a profound impact on the school and on the lives of many hundreds of boys. A bachelor, with ginger hair, round wire spectacles, baggy suits, and teeth stained yellow by his constant pipe smoking, he was probably best remembered for his laugh. It began as a 'hee, hee, hee' which gradually built up steam into a series of snorts, accompanied by a further reddening of his already red face. He was a disciplinarian, but also a man of great compassion and

concern for each individual pupil. He spent school holidays visiting the far-flung homes of schoolboys – though not quite so far-flung as Marsabit. One of the best lessons he taught us, by example, was that all people are equal – not a commonly held view-point in colonial Kenya. He would often be seen out in the school compound, shoulder to shoulder with African ground staff, digging, or shifting stones. He was mocked for it, behind his back, by some staff and boys, but far from demeaning himself his willingness to roll up his

Philip Fletcher (Jake), headmaster of the Prince of Wales.

The main quadrangle of the Prince of Wales school.

sleeves gave him, in the eyes of most, dignity and respect. Jake was, in every sense of the word, a great man. Self-effacing, quite shy, he was nevertheless an inspiring man, who encouraged us in all that we did, whether in the classroom or on the playing field or socially, to live out the school motto 'To the Uttermost'.

A high-light of our first year at the Princo was Jake's 'special lecture', awaited with great anticipation. He felt it his duty, as head, and though a bachelor, to instruct us in sex education. He spoke candidly, and had no qualms whatever about setting sex education in the Christian context of marriage and life-long faithfulness. When it came to question time he fielded well such eager questions as 'How long does it take, Sir?' and 'How often do people do it, Sir?' I did wonder how he knew the answers to such questions, but he had obviously done his research. His usual subjects were maths and mechanics, which he taught with great energy and enthusiasm, and lots of 'hee-heeing'. Mechanics was in his genes, his father having been the inventor of Fletcher's Trolley, used to measure acceleration and momentum.

Our teachers rejoiced in a variety of imaginative and descriptive nicknames. There was 'Dudu' (insect), 'Amoeba', 'Pussy', 'Whiskers', 'Peg-legs', 'Stalky', 'Liversausage' and, most elaborate of all, 'The

Galloping Tapeworm' and 'the Missing Link'. As mentioned, some had been in the War, and had had horrific experiences. Stalky had been commander of a tank regiment, and had been blown up in his tank. The pain of a resulting back injury caused him to pace continuously up and down the classroom, hence his nickname. 'Willy Mac', a dour Scot who was to become my revered housemaster and sixth form physics teacher, had been tortured in a Japanese prisoner of war camp. His fingers and nails were deformed and gave him pain – probably nothing compared with the mental pain of the memories. Peglegs had (not surprisingly) two wooden legs – not, we were given to understand, a result of war, but rather from an injury sustained when working as a missionary in China before the war.

Whiskers taught chemistry, and was famed for his parsimony. He doled out microscopic amounts of chemicals for experiments. There was a famous occasion when he himself broke that fundamental rule of chemistry which he had instilled in us – in order to dilute a concentrated acid always add acid to water, never water to acid. In a moment of aberration he added water from a tap to a flask of concentrated sulphuric acid. There was a violent reaction, and acid sprayed across his arm. His instant response was to douse his watch under the tap. His arm had to wait. A watch cost money; an arm would heal. At least his aberration helped us to remember the rule that he broke.

Some teachers were more susceptible than others to the merciless pranks of us boys. One such was our French teacher, the Galloping Tapeworm – an apt description of the undulating movement of his thin torso. The outer door handle of his classroom had been doctored so that it could easily be removed. If he left the classroom for any reason during a lesson we would remove the outer handle, so that he could not re-enter the classroom. We would then lean with apparent intense concentration over our books. On his return we pretended not to notice his surprise at finding the handle missing – again. Our concentration was such that we did not hear his knocks, his pleas, or notice his plaintive face and gesticulations through the classroom window. After considerable delay we would suddenly notice him, and with profuse apologies, and remarks about the fascination of our French work and the generally poor state of the school's door handles, we would let him back in to his own classroom. Meanwhile we would have glued his blackboard rubber to the ledge. A hole in the wooden wall immediately behind his desk neatly accommodated the nozzle of a very long hosepipe which the groundsmen used to water the playing fields. Their habit was to turn on the tap before going in search of the end of the hosepipe. We would meanwhile have wedged that end in the strategic hole. A sudden jet of water hitting the Galloping Tapeworm full in the back in the middle of a lesson would herald, by several minutes, the arrival of the groundsman.

Driven, I think, almost to suicide by us was Ma R, our English teacher. In wet weather we would deliberately gather clods of thick, glutinous red mud on our shoes, and tramp it into her classroom. 'Out! Out!' she would shriek, whereupon we would obediently leave the classroom and gather more mud. A boy who sat at the back of the class would sometimes start to whistle softly and tunelessly. Every time she looked up he was the picture of innocence, bent over his work. Then, following another burst of whistling, he would climb on his chair, lean out of the window, and shout, as though to a groundsman, 'Hey! *Wewe! Usipige kalele!*' ('Hey! You! Stop making that noise!'). For a while the whistling would stop. And then the process would be repeated. I did actually feel sorry for Ma R. At times our cruelty reduced her to tears.

In those colonial days we whites were unashamedly patriotic to Britain. The Empire, though in its dying days, still evoked a sense of pride. A certain amount of pomp and ceremony was written in to the school routine. Each evening at 6PM the union jack would be lowered at the flagpole in the main school quadrangle. A bugler would sound 'Sunset'. Wherever we happened to be on the school compound, whatever we were doing, when we heard the sound of the bugle we were required to stop, turn towards the flag, and stand to attention until the strains of the bugle faded away. And we were proud to do so. It was a mark of respect to our young Queen. On Saturdays school assembly occurred, not in the school hall, but in the main quadrangle. We all stood, in house groups, around three sides of the square. Then in marched the bugle band, the drum major, a senior boy, proudly twirling and tossing his mace. Jake would take the salute, and the union jack would be raised. Speech days were always accompanied by a march past of the Combined Cadet Force and the bugle or brass band. I watched with envy the trumpeters, and when a vacancy arose for a boy to learn the trumpet I jumped at it. Sadly permission was not forthcoming – lessons involved cost, and our parents just did not have the financial wherewithal. It was part of the cost of being a mishkid. Dennis, likewise, had applied for tennis coaching, but he was told by the school that, as mishkids, our school fees were subsidised, and that if our parents could afford the money for extras like tennis, then they could afford to pay school fees. So no tennis for Dennis. Either way we couldn't win.

1954 saw my entry into Intermediate House. It was altogether happier than Junior House had been. The direst punishment here (apart from the cane) was to have to collect thirty grasshoppers before breakfast to feed the prefects' pet hedgehogs. I was now at the age when we were encouraged, almost expected, to prepare for confirmation. We had a number of classes with the school chaplain, Canon Capon (who had been Dad's best man, and who was the father of my classmate Tim). I learned the commandments off pat in the words of the Authorised Version of the Bible. We went through the catechism, and I was duly presented for confirmation in All Saints' Cathedral by Dad's friend, Bishop Leonard Beecher. I did not feel any different after being 'done'. For many of my contemporaries it was a meaningless ritual.

Crusaders I did enjoy, mainly for the tea. Nairobi Crusader Class, the largest in the world, owed its existence to three doctors – Dr Jarvis, an ENT consultant; his brother-in-law Dr John Winteler, a chest physician; and Dr Doug Calcott, an eye specialist, later to become Dr Jarvis's son-in-law. Those three doctors hired buses from the Kenya Bus Company every Sunday afternoon to ferry boys from the Prince of Wales and Duke of York Schools to Nairobi arboretum, where they hired the scout hall. Meanwhile more buses ferried girls from the Kenya High School for Girls to a separate girls' class run by Mrs Jarvis. Hundreds of boys attended those Boys' Crusader classes over the years. The attraction was the magnificent tea, prepared each week by the Jarvis family. We also had a time of worship, and a talk by one or other of the doctors, and a time of games or a film after the tea. The unashamed aim was evangelism – to bring school children to a Christian faith, and to build them up in that faith. Many Christians owe their faith to that early influence. I personally am hugely indebted to Crusaders, and to those three doctors who gave of themselves and their money unstintingly. Up until 1954 I did not seriously question my beliefs. I knew that the teaching we had in Crusaders was in line with my parents' beliefs. I knew that they were glad that I went to Crusaders, and I was happy to go. It was what one did, as a mishkid. Then a challenge and a change came from a completely unexpected direction.

CHAPTER THIRTEEN

Moral Re-Armament, or MRA, was in its hey-day in 1954. It was a movement founded by an American Lutheran, Frank Buchman, and, in post-war America and Europe, it called people back to spiritual values and Christian ethics. It proposed four Absolutes as aims to aspire to – absolute purity, absolute unselfishness, absolute honesty and absolute love. In the early days of MRA these teachings were closely linked with the Christian Gospel. In time, however, the 'absolutes' became an end in themselves, attained by striving rather than by God's grace. It became more an ethical than a Christian movement. It so happened that our school chaplain, Canon Capon, and the head, Jake, were ardent followers of MRA. It was therefore not surprising when, in 1954, a series of 'special talks' about the Christian faith were announced, that the speaker was to be a local vicar, the Reverend Silberbauer – a high churchman and a follower of MRA. In both respects this was a stance far from that taken either by my parents or by our Crusader leaders. I decided, however, to go along and see what he had to say.

I was taken totally by surprise. The Reverend Silberbauer never mentioned MRA, and he went straight to the core of the Christian faith. He spoke about the cross, and forgiveness through God's grace, and the possibility of new birth, new life, in the power of the Holy Spirit. I had heard it all before, many times. I had, in effect, been immunised by repeated doses of the Gospel. But somehow now it all came over in a new and fresh way. This wasn't head stuff, it was heart stuff. The message of the cross wasn't something warmly to approve, but to be radically challenged by. It meant change. It meant turning the world – my world – upside down. As a mishkid I had been drifting along on the tide of my parents' faith. But this wasn't about my parents. It was about me. What had I done about it – or, rather, what had I let God do about it in me? Mr Silberbauer invited anyone who wanted to talk more, but in private, to come to see him in Jake's sitting room – the very same room where I had been interviewed by the CID officer the previous year. I went, and there, on my knees, without any drama, I did the simplest yet profoundest of things – I asked Jesus Christ to be my Saviour, and committed my life to Him. It is difficult to express in words the effect of doing that. Elation, joy, a profound inner peace. Perhaps for me one of the most significant emotions was a feeling of release from the dirtiness and guilt that had hung over me when I was last in that room. It was now past and dealt with. I had laid all at the foot of the cross, and I had been set free. I remember my walk back to the dormitory in Intermediate House. I felt I was walking on air. And I wondered how on earth I was going to live this out amongst my school friends.

The first decision I made was that I must not be ashamed to pray. Until now I had, when I remembered to, gone through the motions of nightly prayer, but in bed, and unknown to anyone else. In future I must take courage. So I took courage, but very cautiously! I waited until after lights out, then very slowly eased my legs over the side of the bed to kneel. But a full moon let me down. A whisper was passed up the dormitory. 'Webby's praying!' A shoe landed on me, then another. It was a short and distracted prayer that night. But I persisted each night, and the others got used to my eccentricity. Our beds were allocated alphabetically, and I had Walker to one side of me and Wells to the other. After a week or two they asked me why I did it, and I told them as best I could what had happened to me. They wanted to know more. I asked the housemaster, who was none other than the chaplain, if we could meet in his house. He was hardly in a position to refuse, and he made a room available to us. Before long we were about eight boys, reading the Bible together, and praying. It was all very tentative and amateurish, but it was real.

My confirmation took on new meaning for me. Even school chapel services came alive. And Crusader classes helped my faith to grow and mature. I took courage to invite friends to Crusaders – and Mrs Jarvis's teas provided an excellent reason for them to accept. My best friend John came along. He could see that there was something in this Christianity thing, though at the time he was not convinced. It was later, when he joined the RAF, that it all fell into place, and he became a Christian. The groundwork had been done in Crusaders. Another friend, Tom, was an Austrian whose parents had settled in Tanganyika. He was a victim of relentless teasing and bullying, and I felt sorry for him. He too came to Crusaders, and in due course became a committed Christian. It was many years later that I discovered what I never knew at school – Tom was a Jew, whose parents had fled from Nazi occupied Austria. He now heads up a Christian mission to Jewish people.

The year 1954 saw a big change for Dad. Ever since the war he had had the dual role of heading up the mission at Marsabit whilst also having responsibility, as BCMS Field Secretary, for all the other missionaries and missions in East Africa. It involved him in thousands of miles of travel over rough dirt roads each year. It was impossible to fulfil both roles properly. In 1954 his Field Secretarial duties were taken over by Major Sellwood, a retired gentleman who was based in Nairobi. Eric could now concentrate more on the work in Marsabit. We looked forward to spending more time with him in the holidays.

Travel to and from Marsabit was affected by the Mau Mau emergency. All travel through Kikuyu country – the first one hundred and twenty miles of our journey – carried a risk. Dad, on principle, and against advice, refused to carry a gun. We did not stop at all on that leg of the journey. There had been occasions in the past when we had spent the night camping in the Kikuyu reserve. On one occasion it was because of the car breaking down. On another we had run out of time, and just pulled in at the roadside and put up our camp beds – as we would in the NFD. On waking in the morning we found we had camped at a bus stop. We were surrounded by scores of curious onlookers, waiting to take their goods to market on the early bus. It was now out of the question even to travel that section of the road after dark. On one of their journeys to Nairobi Mum and Dad needed to divert to Nyeri, at the foot of the Aberdare mountains. There were two possible routes, and they decided on the spur of the moment to take the longer but smoother road. At the same time that they were travelling their longer route, a white settler took the shorter route. On coming round a bend he met a tree felled across the road. As he screeched to a halt he was set on by terrorists and hacked to death. Even the stretch of road northwards from Nanyuki to Isiolo was not safe. We passed each time the farm gateway where the father of one of our fellow school boys had been murdered. And further on, at the Ngare Ndare escarpment, we passed the burnt out remains of a police post which had been wiped out by Mau Mau. We always felt a sense of relief when we passed the barrier at Isiolo, and entered the safety of the NFD. The fierce northern frontier tribes had no time whatever for the Kikuyu people, and would have given short shrift to any gangs straying into their territory.

At Marsabit life was largely unaffected by the emergency. With more time now available, Dad began once more to make safaris to Boran *manyattas* on the lower slopes of the mountain. In holiday time we were able to accompany him. We would pack our tent, bedding and food and water supplies onto the back of a hired camel. While the camel with its owner followed, we would ride ahead on our ponies and rendezvous with the camel at a specified *manyatta*. A *manyatta* comprised a collection of

Boran woman outside her home.

Boran chiefs.

Boran man.

temporary dwellings, a nomadic village, suited to the migratory lifestyle of the Boran people, as they followed grazing and water supplies with their cattle. Several dome-shaped grass and stick huts were surrounded by a thornbush fence. Within the compound would be a further enclosure for the cattle and goats at night. They were thus doubly protected from lion or other predators, the cattle being the people's wealth, their bank balance, their insurance, their food supply. During the day the young men would take the cattle out into the bush to graze, sometimes many miles from the *manyatta*. At dusk, as the orange ball of the sun sank behind the thorn trees, the trail of cattle would return to the safety of their enclosure. Their arrival would be heralded by a cloud of dust, and a soft lowing, as they called to their calves within the *manyatta*. Once safely inside their enclosure the women of the village would call the cows one by one, by name, to be milked. A cow would prick up its ears at the sound of its name, and push its way through the herd to present itself to its owner.

The dome-shaped huts had just one low entrance, and no windows. They were dark, and the walls blackened by smoke from the perpetual fire burning at the centre of each hut. The eyes had to adjust to the dark interior. The floor would be hardened earth. A raised bed of sticks, covered by cowhide, would be the sleeping area for the family. Gourds and leather vessels, decorated with beads and cowrie shells, would hang from the walls. A blackened saucepan or two would sit by the fire, and a goat kid or young calf might be tethered to the wall. A man might have several wives – as many as he could afford. Each wife, with her children, would occupy a separate hut, and the husband would rotate between his wives. Men wore a *woya,* a white cloth, and turban. The women wore skins decorated with cowrie shells, originally brought from the coast by traders as currency.

It was here, next to such a *manyatta,* that we would camp for several nights. The air would be filled with the acrid smell of wood smoke mixed with cow dung. Flies abounded, and I became an adept fly swatter. The aims of these safaris were threefold – to befriend the people, to provide basic medicines, and to preach the Gospel message. For Dennis and me it was an adventure. It was on these safaris that we learned to drink the Boran delicacies of *ititu* and *buna. Ititu* was simply rancid, smoked milk. The milk, in a smoked skin vessel or gourd, was allowed to go thoroughly sour, drowned flies were scooped out by hand, and the thick, curdled liquid passed around the assembled company in the common vessel. *Buna* appealed to us more. It consisted of roasted coffee beans (a valued import from the Ethiopian highlands) floating in a mixture of sweetened milk and fat. The technique was to take a swallow of the liquid together with a few beans. The latter were then stored in the cheek, and chewed at leisure while the gourd continued its round of the hut.

We would be up early, with the dawn chorus, as the cattle were led out to pasture. Dad would pass the day chatting to the people of the village as and when they were free from their daily chores. He treated simple conditions – conjunctivitis, sores, diarrhoea, malaria. He taught children the basics of reading, hoping to give them an appetite for school. He taught them Christian songs, playing along with his concertina. He listened to their stories, and learned about their customs. He told them of a God of love, not fear, who sent His Son to live and die among us. In the heat of the day, when even the flies were having a siesta, we would all collapse onto our camp beds, in the shade of the tent. In the cool of

Eric treating eye infections.

Gathering outside the tent to listen to the gramophone.

David learning to shoot straight with the ·22

the evening we might venture out into the bush with the shotgun or ·22 to bag a guinea fowl or spur fowl for our dinner. It was here that I learned to shoot straight. After dark, when the people of the manyatta had drawn the thorn bushes across the entrance, and quiet had descended, we would sit around the hissing pressure lamp in our tent and play card games or chess. It was a precious time. We had Dad to ourselves. The constant demands of the mission, and of people, could not distract him. The whoop of a distant hyena, or the grunt of a lion on the prowl, would carry on the night air. And we in our tent felt safe and snug, and in the best place on earth.

Dad had originally been the first person to put the Boran language into writing, and to work out a vocabulary and grammar from scratch. He was fluent in the language, and he was also very knowledgeable about Boran customs. The most important and elaborate of their customs was the seven-yearly Gadamoji ceremony, when an age group

Men undergoing the Gadamoji ceremony.   Gadamoji candidate.

entered adulthood. Dad was at that time the only white person to have been allowed to witness the ceremony. He was visited at the mission one day by Joy Adamson, of *Born Free* fame. This was before the days of Elsa, when Joy Adamson was commissioned to paint portraits of all the tribes of Kenya in their varied tribal and ceremonial attires. She was anxious to paint Boran in their Gadamoji dress, and to find out more about the ceremony. She sat for ages, talking non-stop, listening little, with one of Mum's very best teacups perched at a precarious angle on her lap. But Dad was able to arrange for her to witness part of a Gadamoji ceremony, and to get her painting. When she later wrote about the visit in her book, *The Peoples of Kenya,* she said that she visited the local missionary to find out about the ceremony, but he dismissed her with the statement that 'he was not interested in pagan ceremonies'. Such is the deceit, perhaps jealousy, of those who crave fame.

A safari that we made as a family, further afield, was to North Horr, an oasis on the edge of the Chalbe Desert to the west of Marsabit. The vehicle track down the lava rock slopes of Marsabit mountain was very rough, but once we reached the desert we could speed across the flat, salt encrusted sand. At one point we came across a line of camels, their legs elongated in the mirage on the desert surface. Perched on each was a man with rifle and bandolier. It was a patrol of dubas, the local tribal police, on the look out for shifta – bands of brigands who roamed the desert areas. North Horr consisted then of the oasis pools, and surrounding doum palms, a fort-like police post, and a Government rest house for visiting officials. This last was to be our accommodation. The heat was intense, and the glare of the desert painful. During the day we did not move far from the thick, cool walls and palm-thatch shade of the rest house. But when the cool of the evening arrived we would venture out to the oasis pool, and watch herds of camels homing in on it across the desert. Here they jostled and bellowed at the water's muddy edge, filling their stomachs with the gallons of water that would sustain them for another eight days. As the sun set, and the camels, their thirst slaked by the brackish water, wandered off again into the desert's vastness, so huge flocks of sand grouse arrived to drink. The clouds of tiny birds whirled and wheeled in the air before landing at the water's edge. This oasis was a meeting point, a life source, for every living creature in the desert. It was what made life in the desert possible. Little then did I imagine that one day I would be returning to this oasis, this desert, this harsh paradise, as a doctor. North Horr would one day become a monthly port of call with the Flying Doctor Service, and there I would hold clinics and be interviewed under a doum palm by a French Television crew. If somebody had told me that back in 1954 I would have laughed in disbelief.

Camels at North Horr oasis.

CHAPTER FOURTEEN

Expeditions to North Horr, and holidays on Mount Kenya or at the coast, were very much the exception. Most of our school holidays were spent at home, on the mission compound at Marsabit – and we were more than happy that that was so. The day at home always began at 7AM, in Mum and Dad's bed, with a cup of tea and home-made ginger biscuits. Dad would already be up and out, and we would hear his voice outside, addressing the mission workmen in Borana. They would be squatting in a group, wrapped in their *woyas,* huddled against the thick mountain mist. Dad would allocate the jobs for the day – firewood to collect from the forest and chop, *'fito'* (saplings) to cut for some new building, long grass to slash to reduce the risk of snakes. When the jobs had been allocated they would have short prayers before dispersing. Then Dad would percuss the rainwater tanks, our only source of water, to estimate the level in them. We would hear his fingers tapping the sides of the tank, and the change in note when he reached the water level. Meanwhile we would be snuggled in the big bed, planning our day.

Often our school holidays began before Mum's little school had broken up. After breakfast she would stride off into

Samuel Shake and Ruby.

Marilyn with Diramu.

the mist to her school. There she would be joined by her teacher colleague, Samuel Shake, an Mteita man from near the coast. Before she reached school age Marilyn was cared for by Diramu, and then Rhoda – two lovely young ladies, who were devoted to her. Marilyn would chatter to them in Borana, a language she spoke as well as, if not better than, English. She endeared herself to all she met. One person whose heart she stole was Sharif Shibley. He was a Muslim mullah, visiting from Wajir, to the east of Marsabit. He asked if he could visit Dad to discuss matters of faith. Dad invited him to stay, and for a week he took up residence in our little guest rondavel. Little Marilyn fell for him – perhaps it was the beard, or the turban, or the white robes. And he fell for her. Several times a day she would knock on the door of his room, calling out 'Sheebley! Sheebley! Come!' Marilyn did her bit to foster good Christian/Islamic relations. Once she was five Marilyn joined Standard

Marsabit School Sports Day.

The pupils of the Marsabit School.

One at Mum's school, before a brief encounter with boarding school at Nyeri, when aged six. We were often home for the school sports day, and Dennis and I became honorary members of Marsabit school for the day, joining one of the three house teams – Arba (Elephant), Nyenca (Lion) or Qeramsa (Leopard). The teams would parade proudly in their sashes, coloured according to the house. A VIP such as the District Commissioner's wife would be there to present the prizes. Sports Day was a big day for little Marsabit school.

The school itself, with its four classrooms, was always bright with colour – Mum was a great one for pictures and charts and visual aids of every kind. The standard of teaching was excellent, and laid good foundations for the future careers of the pupils. At that time the school did not go beyond Standard Four, and pupils then had to go on to Intermediate schools down country. The excellent grounding was often remarked on by subsequent teachers. Mum's reputation as a teacher was enhanced by her reputation as a crack shot. One day a lesson was brought to a sudden end by screams and a panicked rush for the windows by the entire class. A large cobra had slid under the door and into the classroom. Mum ran to the house for the ·22 rifle. The cobra was still there on her return, in the now deserted classroom – not at all a happy cobra. It was of the spitting variety, and therefore dangerous even at a distance. Mum crept into the classroom and climbed onto a desk. The cobra reared and spread its hood in anger. Mum took aim. The cobra shot out two jets of liquid, hitting Mum on the cheek, just below the eyes. She fired – and the cobra collapsed in a writhing heap, shot clean through the head. Its venom trickled down Mum's cheeks, and the bitter liquid seeped into the corners of her mouth. An inch higher, and the venom would have temporarily blinded her. There was great jubilation among the pupils as she carried out the now dead snake. As always she made light of her triumph – after all, shooting a cobra is all part of a day's work for a headmistress.

Many of the school pupils were also members of the Sunday School. About sixty boys and girls met in the mud and thatch church on a Sunday afternoon. They loved to have a good sing, and to hear Bible stories, illustrated by flannel graphs which Mum and Dennis and I had laboriously coloured and cut out and pasted to flannelette backing. Every now and then there was a Sunday School outing. Mum and Dad would hire a lorry, and take the Sunday School members (together with unexpected new members, who suddenly materialised on the day) to some beauty spot on the mountain. We loved those occasions.

It was one such time. We children all crammed onto the back of the lorry, Mum and Dad and the driver into the cab. Health and safety was not a consideration. We set off with a roar and a shout, clinging to one another as we swayed down the track. We were going to Lake Paradise, deep in the forest. For an hour the lorry ground its way in low gear up and down the forest track. At times we had to divert round a tree, felled by elephants. In other places we all had to climb off as the driver eased the lorry over rocks and gullies. Suddenly the forest opened up, and there below us was a grassy crater, about half a mile across. It had once been a crater lake. It is a lake again now. But in the 1950s it had dried up – just muddy puddles in the centre of the crater. The plan of the Sunday School party was to have a game of football in the crater. There was just one snag. Two elephants were grazing right in the middle of the proposed football pitch. We disgorged from the lorry, and shouted and pleaded with the elephants to move. They seemed oblivious to our needs. So Dad got out his shotgun, and fired into the air. That was a language that they understood, and rather grumpily they ambled off into the forest. The football game commenced. But not for long. Suddenly a massive rhino and her baby emerged from the forest edge at a trot. They headed straight for the players. There was panic. Everyone headed for the nearest tree, and it was a case of every boy and girl for themselves. They were scrambling over one another. The rhino seemed confused, and with its poor eyesight probably had no idea of the rumpus it had caused. Another shot in the air from Dad, and mother and baby rhinos diverted back into the forest. There was great merriment as people accused one another of having panicked most. Those highest up the tree sheepishly climbed down. The game resumed, with extra time for rhino disruption added at the end. And so at last the sun began to sink behind the crater edge. We all wearily clambered back onto the lorry. Someone started to sing, and soon another then another joined in. Before long we were all in full chorus – except for the little ones, lulled to sleep by the swaying of the lorry.

Christmas and Easter were always special occasions. The church would be decorated with sprays of bougainvillea, the services packed out, with everyone in their best clothes. The birth of Jesus, the resurrection

Rethatching the church.

of Jesus, were times to rejoice and celebrate. But no festival was more colourful than Harvest. After all, life for the people of Marsabit centred on their harvest. Life depended on their harvest. No crops = no food = famine. Good crops = enough food to last the dry season = life. The church was decorated for harvest with sheaves of maize and banana leaves. Some harvest offerings were brought in advance, and laid at the front of the church. Piles of yellow maize cobs, pawpaws, bunches of bananas, sweet potatoes, eggs, live chickens. Outside the church a goat or calf might be tethered. The church bell – the piece of railway line – would clang out. The church would fill, many bringing their harvest gifts with them. Mum would strike up the first hymn on the little harmonium – *'Midan banani'* 'Bringing in the sheaves'. Then the harvest procession would begin, the Sunday School children carrying their gifts up the aisle between the packed wooden benches to the front of the church. Behind them would come others bearing gifts, then the church elders, then Dad. And always, last and most important in the procession, came our four ducks, furiously gobbling up off the mud church floor any maize seed or other gleanings left by those ahead.

Dennis and David holding a dead baboon.   David and Dennis with Samuel Shake.

David with his pet sheep Curly Wee.

The service was followed by an auction, the proceeds of the auction going to the work of the church. One year I spotted a harvest offering that I fancied – a rather bedraggled and bald hen, lying at the front of the church, its legs tied together with twine. Perhaps 'fancied' is not the right word. It was too scraggy, too wretched, to fancy it. Rather I pitied it. As the hen lay patiently through the harvest service, perhaps wondering with suspicion why it was there, I fixed its beady eyes with mine and did some financial calculations. My pocket money amounted to one shilling. I was prepared to spend that, but would it be enough? The auction began. The turn of my chicken came. It was raised aloft, squawking in the hands of the auctioneer. Nervously I called out *'Shillingi toko!'* All eyes turned to me. Silence. 'Let the boy have it!' said an old man. *'Inguragura! Inguragura! Ya guragure!'* intoned the auctioneer. The chicken was mine, unopposed. I carried it lovingly to the house, chicken fleas and all, where it became a member of our extended family – which included my pet sheep Curly Wee.

Another family member was Daigo. She was a baby baboon. Her mother was speared to death when she raided a nearby *shamba,* and little Daigo was found clinging to her back. She was brought to us, and, much as we disliked baboons her little face and wide, pleading eyes were irresistible. We bottle fed her, and she lived at the end of a long rope, tethered to one of our verandah posts. She loved to climb into the roof of the verandah, and scamper along it, her ropy tail dangling over the edge of the ceiling. This contributed to a memorable Christmas service. Dad was conducting a service, in English, in our sitting room, for the white Government officials – the District Commissioner, Police Inspector and so on. The first distraction was the migrating organist. Mum was playing the harmonium, which was placed on a rug on the shiny cement floor. Her chair was not on the rug. As she pedalled the harmonium it gradually slid away from her. Between each verse of a rather long Christmas carol she pulled her chair forward to catch up with it. The congregation was mesmerised as she steadily progressed across the room. Meanwhile Daigo (of whose existence the congregation was unaware) chose to dangle her tail over the edge of the verandah ceiling just outside the sitting room. A piece of scraggy rope appeared to be moving spontaneously up and down the length of the verandah. The congregation didn't know which way to look. Migrating musician. Magic rope. Christmas services at the mission certainly kept one entertained. As Daigo grew we knew that we could not keep her. An adult baboon can be very dangerous. I tried to return her to the forest when a pack of baboons was in a nearby fig tree. I held her up for them to see, hoping that they would call her. Instead with one accord and an awful scream the pack leapt down the tree and came towards us. I ran, but Daigo ran faster, and leapt with one bound onto my shoulder, where she clung, terrified. On a later occasion I took her deeper into the forest, and left her, hoping (probably far too optimistically) that a baboon pack would adopt her. She probably met a sticky end, from fellow baboons or leopard.

On returning from school one holiday we heard that an elephant had been shot in the forest not far from the mission. It had been raiding *shambas* and was a threat to humans. The game warden decided that it must be eliminated. Dennis and I went to find the corpse. We needed no directions – the powerful smell of several tons of rotting carcase led us to the scene. The forest undergrowth had been trampled down all around it. Hyenas and jackals had reduced its bulk, but it was still massive. It seemed a sad and ignominious end for this magnificent king of the forest. The tusks had, of course, been removed, but, with hammer and chisel, we set about removing a molar tooth each, which became prized book ends for many years after.

About half a mile into the forest behind the mission was a deep valley, and in the rainy season a stream trickled along the valley floor. An enterprising Water Department official built a dam across the valley, to trap this water, and form a precious water source for the dry season. It was not a big dam – perhaps fifty yards across, and one hundred yards long. But it was deep, and its waters dark, and it was a source, not just of water, but of fun. There we, with our friends, would go to swim. Normally it would not have been safe for children to go so far into the forest unaccompanied. Elephant and buffalo abounded. But Mum and Dad reckoned that in a group, and considering the noise we made, we were safe. Several of our friends learned to swim in that dam. They had little opportunity to learn to swim. There were, of course, no swimming pools for hundreds of miles. There were no other dams. Lake Rudolf lay one hundred miles away, beyond the desert – and anyway was full of crocodiles. So that small dam in the forest was unique. We spent many happy hours on its muddy banks. We built a raft from a crate and jerry cans. Unfortunately the jerry cans leaked and the raft sank. Then one night it began to rain, and it continued all night. It poured. It deluged. Above the sound of the rain beating on the corrugated iron roof of our house we heard another sound. A deep roar. It came from the forest, from the direction of the valley and the dam. Five inches of rain fell that night. In the morning we could still hear the roar in the forest, and we went to investigate. The valley floor was a raging torrent of water, and where the dam had once been stood a gaping space. The wall had gone. Our swimming days were over.

At the dam in the forest.

In the forest.

CHAPTER FIFTEEN

The Easter holiday in 1956 seemed no different from any other. It was the year that Dennis was due to sit, in the December, the Cambridge Higher School Certificate. I was due to sit School Certificate. So we both had school work to do in the holidays. But there was plenty of time for fun, and we roamed barefoot with our friends. One holiday project was to build a tree house, in a wild fig tree. Apart from when I accidentally dropped a hammer onto the head of Andarea below, giving him a nasty headache, it was a happy and successful project. We could not imagine life without Marsabit. We did know however that change was coming. In the January, which happened to be the twenty-fifth anniversary of Dad's arrival in Marsabit, his old friend Leonard Beecher, now Bishop of Mombasa, approached him with a new challenge. Would he leave Marsabit, and take on the role of Senior Chaplain to Kenya's Prisons Department? At the time, apart from the normal prison population, there were forty thousand Mau Mau detainees held in detention centres around the country. These needed to be rehabilitated and restored to the community. Yet there was no organised, colony-wide chaplaincy service, either to the prisons or the camps. Groups such as MRA and the Navigators were working in some of the larger detention camps. But the effectiveness of some rehabilitation work had been questioned. Bishop Beecher deemed Dad to be the right person to remedy the situation. Dad told us that he had accepted the new challenge, on condition that BCMS could find a replacement for him in Marsabit. It was considered that the church was not yet quite ready to stand on its own feet, without a missionary. BCMS recruited a bachelor clergyman, the Reverend Bernard Brown, for Marsabit, but at the same time our former cook, Petro Oce, was ordained as the first local priest. The aim was, eventually, to make the church independent of missionaries.

Our holiday came to an end. We knew that Dad would soon move to Nairobi, but the plan was that Mum would stay on for a while in Marsabit, to oversee the school until some other satisfactory arrangement could be made. We fully expected to be back in Marsabit for the August holidays, and that was our thought as we packed our school trunks, and loaded the car, and set off down the rough track from the mission. Perhaps it was as well that we did not know that we would not return to our mountain home – at least not for many years. And by then the mission would have moved down to the administrative centre of Marsabit. By then our rambling mud home, and all the other mission buildings – the school, the dispensary, the stone house, the lines, the church – would have been razed to the ground. By then Mum's precious garden, with its flowering shrubs and fruit trees, would have gone wild. The mission compound would have been reclaimed by the forest, and reoccupied

Dad meeting his successor, the Reverend Bernard Brown.

Our last school holiday in Marsabit.

by its inhabitants – elephants, and buffalo, and kudu, and troops of baboons. If we had known that then, I think my heart would have broken. Sometimes it is better not to know.

In his early months in his new job, based at the Kenya Prisons headquarters in Nairobi, Dad was accommodated by kind folk. Initially he had a room in the home of Dr and Mrs Henderson. But then one of my Crusader leaders, Dr Jarvis, said he was going on home leave for several months, and offered their house. It was there that we spent the August holiday, and Mum joined us from Marsabit. It was kind and generous of the Jarvises, but Nairobi was not Marsabit. We felt constricted. We missed our African friends. I do recall though that it was at that time, aged fifteen, that I was first smitten by love. We drove out to Langata, on the outskirts of Nairobi, to the home of a training officer in the East African Posts and Telegraphs Department. Mum and Dad were hoping that he would take a lad

The family at Dr Jarvis's house, Nairobi.

from Marsabit school for training in his department. All that faded into insignificance, as far as I was concerned, when I saw the officer's daughter. A bit younger than me, she was pretty, barefooted, friendly and carefree. I suddenly found to my surprise that my heart was racing, there was a tightness in my throat, I was lost for words and covered in confusion and shyness. What was this weird feeling? I couldn't keep my eyes off her, and when we went home I couldn't stop thinking about her. And yet I don't suppose that she was even aware of it. I never saw her again, but I discovered that day that girls were perhaps more interesting than I had previously thought.

The Jarvises had two houses in Nairobi – one in the city, where we spent the August holiday, and one at Spring Valley, on the outskirts of Nairobi. When they returned from leave they offered us the Spring Valley house to stay. It was a large, rambling house, with a wild, terraced garden, leading down to a stream in the

The Spring Valley house.

valley bottom. Here we spent the next two holidays, and Mum joined us from Marsabit. It was about six years since her diagnosis with breast cancer, and unknown to us it had recurred. She was strongly advised by her surgeon to fly to England for radiotherapy and for the only anti-oestrogen treatment then available – removal of ovaries. Mum was stubborn, and she said no. The surgeon pleaded. She said she couldn't afford the time or the fare. Dad called in help. A family friend and ENT consultant, Theo Goodchild, lived just doors away. He came round and in tears begged Mum to comply with medical advice. And she finally agreed. It was in the Spring Valley garden that she broke the news to us. We had never known, until then, that she had had cancer. We knew she had had a mastectomy, but had always been led to believe that the lump proved to be benign. Now the truth was out. It seemed that our safe and stable home life, epitomised by Marsabit, was falling apart. Mum flew to England alone, to the Royal Marsden Hospital. One of Mum and Dad's war-time friends, a doctor in the army whom

Seeing Mum off at Eastleigh Airport, Nairobi, for treatment.

they had befriended and hosted in Nairobi, reciprocated the hospitality. Dr and Mrs Blakely opened their home in Southgate to Mum, and were kindness itself throughout her treatment.

Aunt Edith and kind friends helped care for Marilyn in Mum's absence. Dennis and I were busy at school, preparing for our important exams in the December. Meanwhile a school project had been launched – to build a new chapel, in memory of those former Prince of Wales boys who had given their lives in World War Two and in the Mau Mau emergency. Until then the school hall had served as a chapel. Now we were to have a purpose-built, dedicated chapel. A fund was launched, and parents were invited to donate. For some farming parents it was a difficult time financially. There was a pineapple glut. One parent, a pineapple farmer, said that he could not afford a monetary donation, but would the headmaster like some pineapples to sell to pupils, the proceeds to go to the chapel fund? The head, Jake, readily agreed, and asked him to leave his contribution on the lawn outside his study. Later that day a five ton lorry drew up, piled high with pineapples, and deposited an enormous heap on the grass. They were sold to us for 50¢ each, or three for a shilling. Christmas had come early! At most meals most boys took with them a whole pineapple to eat, to supplement the sometimes meagre school diet. But even that did not dispose of all the pineapples. Almost every bedside locker contained pineapples, awaiting consumption. Shoe lockers were stuffed with pineapples. The whole school reeked of pineapples. Then various bits of apparatus, borrowed from the laboratories, began to appear in lockers – conical flasks, retorts, glass tubing, bottles. There were bubbling sounds, and the prevailing odour began to adopt an overripe, even alcoholic character. That end of term was a particularly happy one, as partially inebriated boys sampled and shared their various pineapple concoctions.

Dennis had started a Christian Union in the school, meeting in a classroom on a Sunday evening. It had the blessing of Jake, and of the chaplain, Canon Capon. Crusaders continued to be an important part of our week, meeting at Nairobi arboretum on a Sunday afternoon. On a wider front there was a mission to Nairobi by two evangelists, Roger Voke and Ken Terhoven. Our Crusader leaders arranged for any boys who so wished to attend these meetings. They were held at a football stadium, and crowds came, black and white. It was the early days of Billy Graham's crusade ministry, and these meetings were in that style. I found the atmosphere, the message, the swelling sound of the crowds singing:

> This is my story, this is my song,
> Praising my Saviour all the day long …

I found it persuasive and electrifying and inspiring. In school Christians seemed to be a small minority, regarded as somewhat eccentric. Here we were reminded that we were not alone. When the invitation came to make a commitment, or a re-commitment, to Christ I

Grigg House, Prince of Wales School.

went forward, with hundreds of others. It was not mass hysteria. I found it helpful to declare my faith openly. To make a stand. The decision I had made privately, two years previously, in the headmaster's study with the Reverend Silberbauer, I could now declare unashamedly in public.

Dennis had had an offer from Fitzwilliam Hall, Cambridge, to read English, starting the following autumn. In the meantime, after Higher School Certificate exams, he would teach at a private preparatory school for white boys, Pembroke House, at Gilgil in the Rift Valley. My sights were still, since the age of four, set on doing medicine. I needed to do well in School Certificate. We both achieved our aims. Dennis was accepted the following year for Cambridge. I declared my intention to study biology, physics and chemistry for Higher School Certificate, with French and English as subsidiary subjects, with a view to applying to medical school in London. When my intentions were made known to the headmaster he summoned me to his study. He foresaw two problems. Firstly, my strongest subjects were the arts. Jake would like me to do English as my main subject in the fifth and sixth forms. He tried to dissuade me from aiming for medicine. I told him that my mind had long since been made up. Medicine had always been my ambition, and it remained so. It was non-negotiable. He accepted this, and said he admired my single-mindedness (perhaps 'stubbornness' was the word actually going through his brain).

In view of that, he said, there was a second problem. The teaching hospital he had in mind for me was St Thomas's, where an ex-Prince of Wales boy was currently studying. But St Thomas's required, for entry for the second MB exam, physics, chemistry and, not biology, but zoology. The Prince of Wales did not offer zoology at Higher School Certificate level, only biology. But, he assured me, there was a solution. Just across the valley lay the Kenya High School for Girls (known to us as 'The Boma'), and they did offer zoology. He would arrange for me to cycle over there several times a week, and join the girls in their zoology classes. I was appalled. The thought of entering that forbidden territory on my own, and facing a class of girls – a gender that I had had little contact with – was terrifying. The confusion, and loss of speech, and shyness that had overwhelmed me in the presence of the posts and telegraphs officer's daughter would no doubt afflict me many times more severely. When

Jake saw that the idea did not appeal, he said that a possible alternative would be to cram zoology 'A' level in London between the end of our school year in the December, and the start of term at St Thomas's the following October. This seemed to me a much better option. But some of my friends were amazed, appalled even, at the missed opportunity. Every now and then a Prince of Wales boy (including on one occasion our head boy) was caught breaking into the Boma. To be actually offered a valid reason, a permit, to enter that paradise, not just once but regularly, and to turn it down flat was to them – well, words failed! Pure and utter stupidity. Some of my friends developed a sudden and belated interest in applying to study medicine, no doubt with the need to study zoology uppermost in their minds.

Bearing in mind my shyness with girls, and total lack of experience in relating to them, I was shocked, but at the same time flattered, to receive a personal invitation to the sixth form dance at the Boma. Although addressed to me personally, the invitation did not say who it was from. I racked my brains. How had any girl at the Boma got to hear about me, and to know my name? Of course acceptance of the invitation was out of the question. I could not dance a step. I would be overcome with confusion, and would make a fool of myself. I politely declined the invitation, making my excuse that I had an exam the following day (which was true, though not the real reason for my refusal). It was years later that I discovered that the sender was Priscilla Cowen, daughter of the former police inspector in Marsabit – Priscilla who would in due course marry my brother Dennis. To this day she has not forgiven my refusal of her invitation, and she assures me that the only reason she chose to invite me was that mine was the only name she knew in the Prince of Wales! I saw my role in our own Grigg House dances as that of gramophone operator (the precursor of a modern DJ). I would tuck myself into a corner of the common room, with the gramophone table firmly placed between me and the rest of the room. By diligently applying myself to the records, and by avoiding eye contact with girls, I felt safe. On reflection it seems sad, and was perhaps a legacy of living in an isolated place in the holidays, and attending a segregated secondary school in the term time. The opportunities to meet girls in a normal and natural setting were very few and far between. Perhaps it was all part of the mishkid syndrome. It was not until I got to London, and medical school, and began to relate to female fellow students, and to female patients, that I began to grow in confidence in the presence of the opposite sex.

CHAPTER SIXTEEN

I was enjoying the Higher School Certificate course. I was now a senior, with privileges. I was studying subjects that I had chosen to study. We had excellent teachers – my housemaster and physics teacher, Willy Mac, with his tortured, deformed hands; Ken Fyffe, late captain in the army, for chemistry; and, joy of joys, 'the Missing Link' for biology. He derived his nickname from his prominent forehead. 'Link', as we called him for short, had imperfect eyesight, so it was possible to get up to all kinds of mischief at the back of the laboratory without him knowing. He had an African laboratory assistant called Alphonse. We used to engage in pitched battles with Alphonse, blowing gobs of chewed blotting paper at one another through glass tubes. Sometimes a missile went astray, and landed on Link's desk, or even hit him. It

The science block, Prince of Wales School.

always puzzled him as to where such an object could possibly have come from. In the event we all fixed our eyes accusingly on Alphonse at the back. One of Alphonse's duties was to cut biological pictures out of magazines, and paste them onto card for displays on the notice board. We persuaded him once that it was the reverse side of the pictures that Link actually wanted displayed, and before long there was an informative display of pictures of royalty and scantily dressed film stars on the biology notice board.

Fish tanks in the laboratory were used to demonstrate the life cycle of the frog. But frogspawn was not readily obtainable. Link made an offer – he would pay a substantial sum to any boy who brought him frogspawn. This was an offer too good to miss. We had no idea where to get frogspawn, but we did know where to get something that looked remarkably similar – pawpaw seeds. They were round, and black, and slimy. We brought Link a jarful of pawpaw seeds, floating in water. He was thrilled, and paid up. The 'frogspawn' was put into a tank, and the process of watching them develop began. Each day Link would gaze at them hopefully through his pebble glasses. But sadly no hatchings happened. No tadpoles emerged. 'They must have been sterile eggs, Sir' we assured him, and he nodded sadly in agreement.

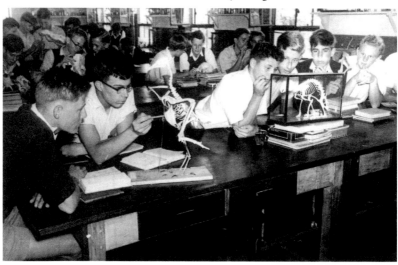

Biology class.

Biology field studies were our greatest joy. We knew that there was a river valley not far from Link's home. We persuaded him on a number of occasions that this would be the best place for a field study. Once in the valley we would disperse in search of secluded spots amongst the reeds to stretch out and sunbathe. Link would turn round from an extended and excited lecture about the larvae of the dragonfly to find that his biology class had dissipated. He would wander forlornly up and down the river, calling us, and in due course we reappeared, full of apologies, to say how we had been diverted by a most amazing insect, which had now flown away, but how about now retiring to his nearby house for a cup of tea? And so we ended up in Link's sitting room, eating his biscuits, and saying how much we appreciated field trips.

I was never particularly good at singing, and I never learned to read music, but I joined the school choir. Bertie Lockhart was our choir master – a short, passionate Scotsman. We entered the Kenya Schools Music Festival, held in the city's National Theatre. The adjudicator was usually imported from Britain. Winners of the various classes gave a concert on the final night to dignitaries, such as His Excellency the Governor, school heads and the adjudicator himself. We won our choir class, but in his comments the adjudicator said that we were 'rather restrained'. He would have liked more gusto. Bertie took his words to heart. At the concert on the final night he concealed behind the curtains on the stage the school's combined brass and bugle bands. When our choir's turn came we let rip, backed up by both bands at full volume. The roof was raised. Gusto was in full gust. The audience, even the Governor and the adjudicator, were convulsed with laughter. The applause was loud and long, and the reputation of the Prince of Wales School for being unrestrained was restored.

A bonus of being in the school choir was that we got to sing Handel's *Messiah*. This was very popular, not so much because boys appreciated the music or the message of the Messiah, but rather because it involved girls from the Boma. Disappointingly all the early rehearsals were separate – tenors and basses at our school, sopranos and altos at theirs. But the time had to come, and it did, when combined rehearsals began. These were times of strutting and preening, when boys and girls self-consciously tried to hide their spots and display their more

The new school chapel. Copyright © East African Standard Ltd.

David supervising the shooting stall at the school fête.

attractive features. Our new school chapel was now complete, and one of the special opening events was to be a performance of the *Messiah*. Unfortunately it was an occasion when many Prince of Wales boys demonstrated their lack of culture and maturity. As the girls launched into the chorus 'For unto us a child is born –' the chapel full of boys dissolved into titters of mirth.

Team sports had never been my forte – my legs of course were the wrong shape. Rugby and football I avoided if at all possible. In cricket my favourite positions were either as scorer, or, failing that, as far out on the periphery as possible, where I could study grasshoppers and ants. I once played for the house first cricket team – there must have been an epidemic of some sort raging, which resulted in desperate choices for the team. I was last man in to bat. We needed one run to draw, two to win. I was out for a duck, first ball. I was not asked to play for the first team again. But one sport I did excel at – rifle shooting. In both ·22 and ·303 competitions I did well. We had a small rifle range at the school, and I was delighted when I was excused the marching and drilling of CCF parades on a Tuesday evening, and was appointed by Captain Ken Fyffe, my chemistry teacher, to be Sergeant i/c Shooting. I was also made captain of the school shooting team, having won the cup for the best shot. This now opened up the opportunity to compete in inter-school shooting competitions, with outings to a large rifle range at Kamiti, outside Nairobi. As a team we did well. In competitions such as falling plates we shot as a team, and had a strategy, and we won. We came back to school proudly bearing our trophies. One unfortunate legacy remains with me until this day – there was no consideration in those days of hearing damage. We fired ·303 rifles with no ear protection, and now we reap the consequences.

Dennis was much better than I was at games, and he also did well in athletics. Sports Day was a big day in the school calendar, with fierce inter-house competition. There were also races for teaching staff and parents, and, most popular of all, for the African domestic staff. With no training and no preparation they ran at a phenomenal speed. Apart from our own sports day another highlight of the year was the Triangular Sports, between the Alliance High School (Africans), the Duke of Gloucester School (Asians), and the Prince of Wales (Whites). Always the results were the same: Alliance High School way ahead as winners, us second and Duke of Gloucester third. It was good and salutary for some of our more racist Prince of Wales boys to be beaten by the Alliance boys: to be reminded that just because they were white they were not superior. In hockey it was usually the Asian boys who won. Sports Day brought the term to an end. The bugle and brass bands would parade across the now empty athletics field, raising the dust with their marching. Silence would descend on the hundreds of pupils, staff and parents. As a lone bugler played *Sunset* the union jack would be lowered. Jake stood there, next to the flag pole, trilby hat in hand, a lone, magnificent figure. And we felt proud to be Prince of Wales boys.

Dad was getting his teeth into his new job. He made a tour of every prison and detention camp in Kenya, to assess the spiritual needs and priorities. One such visit was to Mageta island, in Lake Victoria – a maximum security camp, where 'hard core' Mau Mau were being held. He was warned not to expect any positive response from the detainees. On arrival he sent word that he would be holding a service for any who wished to come. Nearly three hundred turned up. He arranged for a pastor to be posted there as soon as possible. Everywhere he went there was a hunger for books – Bibles, grammars, dictionaries, whatever. Detainees wanted to move on, and to improve their lot in life. He responded.

The most illustrious – or notorious (according to one's point of view) – of the prisoners and detainees that he was responsible for was Jomo Kenyatta. He had been accused and convicted of master-minding the Mau Mau rebellion. This he always denied, and in particular he denied any responsibility for the brutal excesses of Mau Mau. Following his trial at Kapenguria in 1953 he, and five other convicted leaders of Mau Mau, were banished to prison in Lokitaung, in Kenya's remote north-west. In January 1957 Dad made the first of two

Mzee Jomo Kenyatta.

visits to Lokitaung, in his capacity as prison chaplain. He did not know whether any of the prisoners would agree to speak with him, and whether the long and gruelling road journey would have been worthwhile. In the event Jomo Kenyatta and Waruhiu Itote (known as 'General China') were both friendly and receptive, and showed great interest in spiritual matters. The other prisoners were hostile.

In August 1957 Dad made a second visit to Lokitaung. On this occasion he took with him Bishop Obadiah Kariuki. Bishop Obadiah was himself, like the prisoners, a Kikuyu, and was distantly related to Kenyatta. He was the first Kenyan African to be consecrated bishop, and was a much respected, gentle, deeply spiritual man. He had shown enormous courage in speaking out against the atrocities of Mau Mau. An incident occurred on the long journey to Lokitaung. They stopped at the little town of Kitale, in the western highlands – an area populated by many white farmers. The most gruelling part of the journey lay ahead – two hundred and fifty miles of backbreaking road and desert. They needed refreshment, and went into a small café, Kitale Bakery, owned by a white couple. They took a seat, and Dad ordered tea and cakes.

'We can serve you, sir, but not him,' said the owner, indicating Bishop Odadiah. 'We don't serve Africans here.'

Dad was furious, and protested, 'Do you realise who you are talking about? This is Bishop Obadiah Kariuki. He is my superior. How dare you refuse to serve him?'

But refuse they did, and they left, Dad, as it were, shaking the dust off his feet. Bishop Obadiah was much more conciliatory, and wanted Dad to stay and enjoy his tea and cakes. Such was the humility of the man. But Dad was – as always in this sort of situation – both angry and embarrassed. The problem was sorted out by time – the Bakery remained for many years, and thrived, but its white owners moved on, swept away by winds of change. Dad and Obadiah were on a mission that would have a profound effect for good on the nation. The café owners were confined to their small-minded world.

Kenyatta was delighted to see Bishop Obadiah, and was moved to know that his people were praying for him. In the words of Jeremy Murray-Brown's biography of Kenyatta:

He took Kariuki to his cell and they talked alone about the state of their country, and about God's love and mercy for the individual. Kenyatta learned how the Christians had met the Mau Mau and loyalist terror with equal courage. He asked if he could keep the Bible; it was what he wanted most of all, he said, and he planned to read it right through from beginning to end. Kariuki then went to one of the larger rooms to meet the other prisoners. Here his reception was very different. He had journeyed up to Lokitaung with the European prison chaplain. Kaggia at once attacked him for this; Kaggia, the one-time leader of his own sect, declared that there was no point in praying to God. There is no God, he said. Christ is only for Europeans. Kenyatta tried to quieten them, but without success. One by one they all trooped out of the block, leaving only Kenyatta and China to receive Kariuki's farewell prayers … The African bishop's visit was an important episode in Kenyatta's life at Lokitaung. Now he could see more clearly than ever before where his destiny lay. Only he could bridge this divide of bitterness which at present seemed as wide and deep as the Rift Valley itself. *

Dad wrote of that visit: 'I believe Jomo and China to have a new outlook on life, resulting from what might be called a spiritual experience that I judge them both to be undergoing. These were the only two who joined with the Bishop and me in prayer before we left.' Who knows what effect those visits had on Jomo Kenyatta, and so, in turn, on the nation of Kenya, that was to come to birth within a few years?

* Murray-Brown, Jeremy *Kenyatta* (1972) George Allen & Unwin Ltd.

CHAPTER SEVENTEEN

Dad's work as senior prisons chaplain was expanding fast. He had placed a chaplain, church army captain or evangelist in every prison and detention camp in Kenya. He spent much of his time visiting and encouraging them. He was now, for the first time in his life, earning a proper salary – £1,000 a year seemed enormous after the annual mission allowance of £200. He was allocated a government house on the Bernard Estate on the western fringes of Nairobi. But because it was susceptible to flooding he took out a mortgage and bought a neighbouring house instead.

Our Nairobi house before Mum got to work on the garden.

Our Fiat which we called 'Kiroboto' (Swahili for flea).

For the first time ever we were property owners. Mum handed over Marsabit school into the capable hands of her colleague Samuel Shake, and joined Dad in Nairobi. She soon got employment as a teacher at a small primary school at Muthaiga, and Marilyn enrolled at the same school. Marilyn had hated her year as a boarder at Nyeri Primary School, and had felt as lonely as I felt when I started at Nairobi Primary. To live at home and attend the school where Mum taught was, for her, bliss. Mum purchased a little second hand Fiat, with a soft top. It was called *Kiroboto,* the Flea. Life for the family had radically changed. Our normal place of worship became Nairobi cathedral, where Dad had been made a canon. It was a far cry from the little mud and thatch church in Marsabit.

John.

1957 was drawing to a close, and I was still boarding at the Prince of Wales. I had just one year of school remaining. Saturdays at school could be boring – we had morning lessons, a prep session, and then the day was free. My friend John and I used to cycle rather aimlessly round the large school compound, which we were not allowed to leave (Mau Mau still being a potential threat). We would often end up at one of the three school entrances, watching traffic on the Kabete road. John was an expert on makes of car, and we would see how many we could spot, and dream of the day when we might own a Mercedes. It was such a Saturday, sitting at the entrance to the jacaranda-lined main drive, when I suddenly realised that I could almost see our new house, just two miles away. Here I was filling in time at school, bored, and just down the road was home, with Mum and Dad and Marilyn doing their things. I had a sudden longing to be with them. Never before had home been so close, and yet so unattainable. I decided there and then that I wanted, for my final year at school, to become a dayboy – or, as the boarders would call me, a despised 'day bug'. Dennis's departure to England and Cambridge in the August of 1957 had made me realise what a final and drastic separation that had been. It would be my turn in a year's time, and who knows when I would see home and parents again after that? I wanted just one year of home life before leaving for England. At the next opportunity I told Mum and Dad of my wish, and they were all in favour. Much less in favour was my housemaster, Willy Mac. He had me lined up to be head of house. He did his best to persuade me to board, but to no avail. It was a decision I never regretted.

The day Dennis flew to England.

An action I did regret, often, was the burning of all Dad's diaries and letters, dating back to his arrival in Marsabit in 1931. He had kept them in a trunk in Marsabit – a priceless record of those early days. Every letter written to his parents he had carbon copied and kept. Every diary entry was there – the excitements, and challenges, and set-backs of those early days in Marsabit. How he had to learn the language by signs and pointing, and how he gradually worked out the grammar of the as yet unwritten Borana language. How the elephants rubbed against his flimsy grass hut. How the first Christians came to faith. When we moved into our small Government-provided house in Nairobi there was just not room for all the stuff from our rambling home in Marsabit. Dad asked me to take the trunk of his memoirs, and burn the contents. I lit a bonfire in the garden, and sat for hours, reading, burning, reading, burning. As the last pages were consumed by the flames it dawned on me what a terrible thing I had done. I had burned irreplaceable memories and records. I had burned the story of a life. It was sacrilege. But it was too late. I vowed always in future to treasure people's memories; to value the written record; to hand on the past to future generations.

Mwangi, a detainee at a detention camp.

On one of his visits to a large Mau Mau detention camp at Mtito Andei Dad had been accosted by one of the detainees. It was Mwangi, an old friend who had worked for many years at the CMS guest house in Nairobi. Mwangi had been arrested during a massive security operation in Nairobi, Operation Anvil. Something incriminating had been found in his house, possibly planted there. Now he was preparing for release. Dad kept in touch with him, and on his release he came to work for us as house servant and cook. In the years ahead, when Dad became increasingly disabled by Parkinsons's disease, Mwangi proved to be such a loyal and devoted friend, tending to Dad's personal needs with tenderness and care. But all that lay ahead. Mwangi only needed part of the servants quarters at the back of our new house. I converted the other part into a study. I would work there in an evening to the smell and sounds of Mwangi cooking his supper of *ugali*, onions and beans next door. I worked very hard during that last year at school, determined to get the exam grades required by St Thomas's Hospital. I was also determined to prove to my teachers that becoming a day boy had not had a detrimental effect on my studies.

That year of living at home was a precious time. Each morning I would cycle to school, my heavy rucksack full of files on my back. In an evening, before getting down to study, there was time to talk about the day with Mum and Dad and Marilyn. I had inherited a love of gardening from Mum, and we would spend time together inspecting the progress of plants. The garden had been a wilderness when we moved in, but it didn't remain that way for long. Mum had green fingers, but also a very wicked streak, which extended to her garden projects. I collaborated in her wicked schemes. We had a bed of canna lilies of every known colour. But occasionally Mum would espy a variety that she had not got. One was in the flowerbed on a roundabout in the centre of Nairobi. We planned a night raid. She drove, I nipped out of the car and dug up a small piece of canna tuber. The raid was over in seconds. The roundabout flowerbed looked no different, and we had another variety to add to the collection. Mission complete! A near neighbour, Dora, had a beautiful garden of which she was very proud and jealous. She would not share plants or even cuttings. Mum offered to care for the garden while Dora was on leave. Once the coast was clear she took cuttings from a number of Dora's plants. They all grew – everything grew for Mum. By the time Dora returned from leave we had a number of 'stolen' cuttings growing profusely in our garden.

'That's a lovely plant, Ruby!' Dora would say, as she looked round our garden. Little did she know that it had originated from her own garden.

'Yes, would you like a cutting Dora?' said Mum generously.

'Oh, yes please!'

The neighbouring house to one side of us was occupied by temporary army families. They had no interest whatsoever in the garden, and it grew wild, and looked unsightly. Hints that they might like to plant some trees and shrubs were ignored. So at night Mum and I climbed over the fence and planted a screen of suitable trees amidst the long grass. On subsequent nights we made further raids to water them. The occupants never seemed to question where this mass of flowering shrubs and trees between their house and ours had sprung from. Dad, the clergyman, would 'tut tut' benignly at our escapades, a twinkle in his eye.

That final school year sped by. Weekends were no longer boring. I joined the All Saints Cathedral Youth Fellowship, run by Sarah White – who subsequently, and happily, married one of my Crusader leaders, Robert Howarth. It was wonderful to see two of my favourite people, both of whom had influenced my Christian life, come together like that. Crusaders continued to be an important part of my life, and I am eternally grateful to the three doctors, Jarvis, Winteler and Calcott, for the inestimable influence they had, not just on my life, but on that of many boys at the Prince of Wales and Duke of York schools.

By now some of our Marsabit friends – in particular Luka Daudi and Kenneth Mude – had gained entrance to the prestigious Alliance High School, near Nairobi. They would come and visit us at our Nairobi house, and it was wonderful to see them and renew friendship. Samuel Shake, now head teacher at Marsabit, came to stay. In that white suburb of Nairobi eyebrows were raised. It was not usual in those days for whites to have Africans to stay. But, then, we were not 'usual'. Conversations with neighbours ran along the lines:

'I see Ruby that you have had a visitor?'

'Yes!'

'A black man!'

'Yes – he is a friend. Mr Shake.'

'I see. But not actually staying with you?'

'Yes, staying. As I say, he's a friend.'

'Oh!'

And so the conversation would end. The winds of change were blowing in 1958, but some people were hiding behind a wind break. Luka, Elisha, Kenneth, Solomon and other friends would emerge

Kenneth and Luka in Nairobi, when they were students at the Alliance High School.

from further education just at the
time that Kenya was preparing for
independence. A crucial time. There
was a need for Africans to take up
posts in the civil service that had
previously been held by Europeans.
Job opportunities were wide open
for suitably educated Africans, and
promotion was likely to be rapid.

Samuel Shake and Luka.

Kenya desperately needed the likes
of our Marsabit friends – not just for their educational achievements, but
for their Christian values of integrity, and justice, and incorruptibility.
Luka rose as high as one can rise in the civil service. He became a
Provincial Commissioner, and his nickname was 'Mr Straight'. Kenneth
became Kenya's ambassador to France and Australia. Solomon worked
for years in the Teachers Services Commission. Elisha became an MP
and then Minister of Transport. Mum was proud of her boys, who
called her 'Mother'. She would have been even prouder if she had lived
to see their success.

Our Higher School Certificate exams took place in early December.
The papers were tough, but we had been well taught, and I was hopeful
of results that would assure my place at St Thomas's. But there was no
time to wait for results. I had to get to England to begin cramming
zoology for the summer 'A' level exams. On 8th December, 1958, just
two days after exams finished, I was booked to fly to England. Mum and
Dad bought me a double breasted grey suit, and a suitcase – which the
Indian shopkeeper jumped up and down on to demonstrate its strength.
I donned thick woollen long johns which Aunt Edith had brought out
from England – my only hope of surviving the winter cold in England,
she assured me. And we drove to Nairobi's brand new Embakasi airport.
I had no idea when I would see Mum and Dad and Marilyn again – we
hoped perhaps in two years time. Here I was, a rather naïve, worldly-
innocent seventeen-year-old, setting off into a far and strange land.
I was leaving behind everything that felt safe, everyone I loved. The
goodbyes were difficult, and as I walked through immigration, and past
the point of no return, I felt unutterably alone.

And then I saw him. Dr John Winteler, my Crusader leader, a large burly bear of a man. He came towards me with arm outstretched. 'What are you doing here?' I asked incredulously.

'The immigration officer is a patient of mine. He let me through. I knew you were leaving tonight, and I thought you might like a bit of company while you wait for the plane.' He stayed with me, such a friend and comfort. And as we were called to board, and he said goodbye, he pressed £10 sterling – a huge sum then – into my hand.

My plane at Embakasi Airport, Nairobi.

CHAPTER EIGHTEEN

An abiding memory of 'Princo' days is that of standing around the piano in the school hall, together with other gawping junior boys, and listening with rapt hero worship to one of the prefects singing and extemporising on the piano. His name was Roger Whittaker, and in due course he would become a world-renowned folk singer. One of the songs that he now sings, a favourite of mine, which never fails to bring a tear, is *My land is Kenya*. It sums up the love, the longing, the passion, the ache that those of us who were born there feel for Kenya:

> My land is Kenya,
> so warm and wild and free.
> Right from the highlands to the sea
> you always stay with me,
> here in my heart; here in my heart.

My land is Kenya. But is it? Where do I belong? Does it belong to me? This is the cry of the mishkid, of the trans-cultural kid. That ambiguity is the legacy of being born abroad of missionary parents. As children we think we belong to the land and to the culture that we are growing up in, then we discover that we don't. When I first arrived in England I suffered from culture shock. What was this drab, cold land? Why did nobody speak to one another? In the underground, on the bus, heads swayed with the rhythm of the motion, eyes fixed glassily ahead, as though it was a land of automatons. I missed the sun, the warmth

– not just of the weather but of people to one another. Why did strangers not greet one another? Where was the *joie de vivre* –or, as they would call it in Kenya, the *furaha?* In those early days in England there was no way in which I felt I belonged here. I talked endlessly – probably very boringly – about Kenya. I sought out those who would understand. Call it homesickness, or grief – it hurt badly. Nobody understood in those days about 'reverse culture shock' and 'transitional' issues. You just had to work it out and work through it.

That is the almost inevitable consequence of being born and bred in a land other than that of one's parents. At the time of Kenya's independence, on 12th December, 1963, I had a choice – to apply for Kenyan citizenship, or remain British. It had to be one or the other. By then I was in my final year of medical studies in London. If I had had that choice five years earlier I am sure that I would have opted for Kenyan citizenship. But by 1963 I had begun to resolve in my mind where I truly belonged. I had been back to Kenya twice, to visit Mum and Dad – in 1960 and 1962. I still loved the land. I regarded myself as a *mwananchi* – a son of the land. I was a son, but not an heir. Kenya belonged to black Kenyans. It was their land, their inheritance, their right. My involvement was, not so

Our last time together as a family in Nairobi, 1960.

much an accident of history, but a transient phase in God's plan for our family. My real roots, my ancestral roots, were in England.

This confusion about where I belonged, the ambiguity of heritage, was probably only finally resolved for me when I returned to work as a doctor in East Africa for nine years. I loved the land as much as ever. I loved the people. But I finally realised that it did not belong to me, and I did not belong to it. I was a foster child of Kenya, a happy and grateful foster child, but not a true *mwananchi*. So did I have qualms about putting my own children through exactly the same experience that I had had? One was born in Uganda, one in Kenya, two in Britain. But all four spent some of their early years in East Africa. Why? Because we, Rosemary and I, like my parents, believed that that was where God wanted us to be. We sent Andrew and Paul to boarding school at an early age – albeit to a much happier and kinder school than I went to. St Andrew's, Turi, was a Christian school, with caring staff, some of whom were our personal friends. Yet even so Andrew and Paul suffered the loneliness and homesickness that I suffered. Their early letters home were sometimes heartbreaking. We felt guilt and shed tears – as my parents did. We questioned whether we were doing the right thing. We still, sometimes, look back and wonder. Yet ask the boys if they would have had it any other way, and they say most definitely not.

Do I, in any way at all, regret my upbringing as a mishkid? If I have one regret it is that I did not have as much time with my parents as I would have wished. For my very early years Dad was away at war. When he returned home in 1945 he was, to me, a stranger. By the beginning of 1948 I was off to boarding school, and from then until my last year at secondary school, I only saw Mum and Dad in the school holidays. And Dad was often busy, with his wide responsibilities as mission Field Secretary. I had that one precious year in the sixth form, living at home. Then I was off to England to study. Two brief visits to Kenya followed during the next four years, during the second of which Dad was diagnosed as having Parkinson's disease, with associated dementia. The next time I saw him, in 1963, was at Heathrow airport, when he was a shrunken, white-haired figure in a wheelchair. He died just after the New Year, 2nd January, 1964. Meanwhile Mum's cancer had returned yet again. Rosemary's and my wedding, in 1964, was about the last time she was able to stand. She died at Easter 1966. Dad was fifty-eight years old, Mum fifty-seven, when they died. The inscription on their gravestone at Hindhead says:

> They gave their lives in missionary service.

I think *gave* is the operative word. They gave totally of themselves: health; comforts; financial security; yes, even family considerations came second to what they believed God had called them to. They lived for good, and they lived for God.

So was I, were we, victims of their calling? Were we cheated out of a 'normal' childhood, a 'normal' home life? I really don't believe so. When God called Mum and Dad to Africa, He indirectly called us – Dennis, Marilyn and me, though then unborn. When God called Rosemary and me to Africa, He indirectly called Andrew, Paul, Stephen and Lynette. We see the process now being repeated in the lives and families of our own children and grandchildren. God does not deal with individuals in isolation. He deals with families. He involves generations as yet unborn. We shared the privilege of our parents' calling.

Was growing up as a mishkid a matter of survival? Of turning out all right 'in spite' of the circumstances? Again, I do not believe so. I am deeply thankful for that upbringing. It taught me about the importance of vocation – that we each have only one life to live, and so how are we going to live it? For ourselves, and our own pleasure and indulgence, or for others? It taught me that God has a plan and purpose for each life, and true fulfilment does not depend on income, or comfort; not on material things or pleasures; but on living that life in line with God's plan. I saw that pattern being lived out by Mum and Dad, and I am grateful. My upbringing taught me that responsibilities in life are more important than rights. We live in a world obsessed with 'human rights'. There is often no counterbalance of 'human responsibilities'. I saw lives lived responsibly and responsively to others. Lives of giving, not taking.

My upbringing taught me to value the simple things in life – home-made toys, and games that involve the imagination and creativity. Family meals around the table, with laughter and sharing of experiences and thoughts. Simple, wholesome food. Contentment with what one has, rather than an acquisitiveness for what others have got – and for what the advertisers keep telling us we need and owe to ourselves. Pleasure in the things around us – the song of a bird, the delicacy of a flower, the smile of a friend, the touch of family, the warmth of the sun – rather than a constant urge to seek new experiences. C S Lewis, in *The Allegory of Love,* writes of 'the quiet fullness of ordinary nature'. He describes the appreciation of simple pleasures as 'the drippings of grace'. Philip Yancey *(What Good is God?)* talks of 'being attuned to the beauty of the ordinary'. It is, of course, not just mishkids who learn to appreciate simple things, but it is one outcome of being a mishkid. As missionaries we possessed little, but we lived among people who often possessed nothing, and that put our lives into perspective.

My upbringing taught me about hospitality, about having an open home – a place where all were welcome, expected or unexpected, at any time of day or night. It taught me that you don't offer the minimum in hospitality. You don't hold conversations on the doorstep, with body language that says 'Go away!' It's the hospitality of the open door, the invitation to 'Come in! Be at home! Take your time!' Many homes in Kenya have no proper door, or, if they do it is wide open for most of the time. So the visitor does not herald their presence with a knock. There are no door bells. The custom is to call out *'Hodi!'* It is an Arabic word that probably means 'Is all well?' The reply from the host is *'Karibu'* (or *'Karibuni'* if there is more than one guest). It means more than 'Come in!' It means 'Welcome!' Mum and Dad entertained anyone and everyone – from Provincial Commissioners to old folk who spat on the cement floor.

My upbringing taught me to value people – not by the colour of their skin, or by their status in society, but by virtue of the fact that God values each individual. I grew up in colonial Kenya. British rule was, in many ways, benign and just, but there was racial divide. Separate schools. Separate hospitals. Separate areas in buses and trains. Separate public toilets. I grew up to believe that this was wrong. Every individual is of equal worth in God's sight. So I grew up with African friends. We played together. We sometimes gathered at night around the pressure lamp and played board games together with our friends. They called Mum and Dad 'Mother' and 'Father'. To them our parents were like their second parents, and we were their brothers. Our home was their home; our family their family. At school Dennis and I refused to use the common derogatory terms for Africans. We called them 'Africans', and were derided for it. We were, whether we liked it or not, bound by a racist system, but we could never be bound by racist attitudes. I am grateful for that upbringing.

Growing up in a foreign country gives one a wider perspective of the world. It makes one very aware that one's home country is not the centre of the world. There are other cultures and languages of great richness and variety. In this day and age of easy and relatively cheap travel many people, of course, get to see all sorts of foreign lands. But it is always from the viewpoint of a tourist. It is hit and run stuff. Warriors dress up for the occasion, putting on a performance in a hotel lobby. Tourists pack into zebra-striped vans, and peer at animals and people from a safe distance. They might even barter for a carved wooden animal, and feel that they have related to the person behind the stall. They think they have seen and experienced 'the real Africa'. But in fact they have only just brushed the surface. We had the enormous privilege of growing up in, of being part of, another culture – of living in it, not peering at it.

Perhaps of all the things that I learned from my upbringing as a mishkid the one that I value most was that of faith. There was always a spiritual dimension to life. Before any journey, we prayed. If there was a problem, we prayed. If life produced a nice surprise, we thanked God. The fact that my parents were Christians did not automatically make me one – as the saying goes, God has many children, but He has no grandchildren. I had to make my own decision about faith. And Mum and Dad never, at any time, pressured us, though I have no doubt that they prayed for us every day of their lives. They set an example by their lives, and I wanted and sought what they had got. There are now four successive generations of 'missionaries' in our family, and I believe that for each generation the 'bug' has been not so much taught as caught.

Missionaries are nowadays increasingly regarded with disapproval – particularly by anthropologists, but often by society at large. They are associated with imperialism, and paternalism, and with the worst excesses of history. Many mistakes have no doubt been made by missionaries, and attitudes have not always been as they should. But an enormous amount of good has been done – pioneering educational and agricultural and medical work, often in very challenging circumstances. Missionaries have contributed enormously to the study and preservation of indigenous languages, and to the understanding of local cultures. Nations have been set on the path towards stable independence by the groundwork done mainly, of course, by the colonial civil service, but supplemented by the contribution of missionaries. The chief contribution of missionaries has been to sow the seeds of the Christian faith. Those who accuse missionaries of exporting a western religion forget that Jesus was a middle-eastern Jew. Christianity has never been a 'western' religion. The vast majority of Christians now live in the non-western world. It is in Africa and China and South America that the Christian faith is exploding, a legacy of mission. Missionaries now come to the west from these dynamic churches, to help and inspire our sad, materialistic, lost society. Now we have their mishkids growing up amongst us – and what do they make of that?

I have had the privilege of being doubly blessed – I have been a mishkid myself, and I have been the parent of four mishkids. I have experienced the phenomenon from both perspectives. There are the obvious downsides – financial and material; separation and isolation; ambiguity of where in the world you belong. But the upsides, in my experience, more than compensate – the fascination of living in extraordinary places; of growing up in another culture; of being part of a bigger world. The satisfaction of being part of something really worthwhile and purposeful. You may not know quite where in the world you belong, but one thing you do know is that, wherever you are, it's where God wants you – and there is no greater joy and security than that.

ACKNOWLEDGEMENTS

I am grateful to those who have encouraged me to write this memoir, and who have read the script, made helpful and wise suggestions, and have weeded out grammatical errors. Special thanks to Jan and Roy Stafford, the Reverend Dr Mary Barr, Dr Chris and Betty Oliver, Trisha Hutchison and Roy Knightley. Above all, thanks to my wife, Rosemary, who is my constant encourager, supplier of cups of coffee, and co-producer of four mishkids.

ALSO BY DAVID WEBSTER

The Shimmering Heat: Memories of a Bush Doctor in East Africa

Printed and Published by Stanley L. Hunt Ltd.

Available from
Dr. D. Webster
The Grange,
Hill End,
Upton-upon-Severn,
WR8 ORN
E-mail: namirembe@btinternet.com